BASIC
CARPENTRY

BASIC CARPENTRY

B.MITCHELL

Published by Marshall Cavendish Books Limited
58 Old Compton Street
London W1V 5PA

© Marshall Cavendish Books Limited 1975, 1976, 1977, 1978, 1979,
1980, 1981,1982, 1983, 1984, 1985

First printing 1977
This printing 1985

Printed and bound by Grafiche Editoriali Padane S.p.A.,
Cremona, Italy

ISBN 0 85685 244 9

This volume is not to be sold in Australia
or New Zealand

Contents

Making a start with softwood

Carpentry is one of the easiest skills of all to learn. It is surprising how quickly the few basic techniques can be mastered and how satisfying and economical it is to build even the simplest of objects. It is really a matter of organizing the tools and materials, then following the directions step by step, carefully and patiently.

Such obscure terms as rabbet plane, spokeshave or ripsaw make woodwork sound much more difficult than it really is. 'Basic Carpentry' sets out to avoid the inhibiting jargon of traditional joinery and to introduce the reader to valuable techniques in a clear and straightforward way. Each technique is related to a specific project, thus enabling you to try it out in practice. Detailed diagrams and full-colour photographs illustrate the steps involved, while the tools and materials needed are given in full.

The pot stand described overleaf is an ideal project with which to begin. With no previous experience of carpentry but a certain amount of care a very satisfying result can be achieved at very little cost. The basic techniques of sawing, cutting and sanding are introduced as

are some of the most important tools. Once you have built the pot stand you will be able to construct a number of other useful things using the same principle.

Softwood

Wood is made up of long tubular cells like a bundle of drinking straws tied together. This structure makes wood much stronger in one direction than the other. It is much easier to cut along the cells or grain (ie to rip) than it is to cut across them (ie to cross-cut). The term 'softwood' does not imply lightness, weakness or unreliability. It refers to the family of coniferous or cone-bearing trees which are non-porous and which have needle-pointed leaves. All broad-leaved, deciduous trees on the other hand—such as mahogany, teak and oak—are classed as hardwood. Most of the timber used for carpentry is of the softwood class as it is sufficiently strong for most purposes and is easily worked on account of its softness and straightness of grain, besides being cheaper than hardwood.

An example is pine, one of the most im-

portant commercial timbers, large quantities of which are imported from Scandinavia. Throughout the world, pine is regarded as the carpenter's standard wood for household fittings and furniture.

Another versatile softwood is western red cedar, which, even left unpainted, does not deteriorate, and is used for complete buildings in some countries. Still further along the spectrum is Douglas fir, the tough, straight-grained and water-resistant species which yields timber for large-scale outdoor construction work and for flooring.

Selecting standard sizes

Most timber merchants or lumber yards hold a large selection of stock sizes. These are usually referred to by their sectional sizes: ie the width by the thickness. For example, you would ask for a 100mm x 50mm (4″ x 2″) piece of pine, 2m (6′6″) long. In this book the millimetres always refer to the sectional size and the centimetres or metres to the length.

The standard sizes refer to sawn wood so when buying prepared (ie planed) wood, the actual size will be fractionally smaller. The size of prepared wood can vary slightly from batch to batch, so always buy enough to complete a project. Select clean, straight pieces and try to look through the stock for those without knots, splits, or discolouration. For most projects any of the softwoods will do.

Tools

There is a great variety of special-purpose tools available. Many of these are for convenience only and most work can be done perfectly well using a minimum number of hand tools. Cutting tools must have a keen edge and are therefore potentially dangerous. Never work on an uneven or unsteady surface: if you do not have a work bench, use a bench hook on the kitchen table.

Saw. There are many sizes and types of hand-saw. Almost any saw will do, but a small, light panel saw or a compass saw with interchangeable blades are both easy to handle and suitable for all small projects.

Carpenter's square. This is used to make guidelines for sawing and chiselling etc. Since it forms a rigid 90° angle its primary purpose is to make lines perpendicular to the edge of the timber for cross-cutting. Use a sharp pencil to mark the line and if you have a trimming knife you can use it to score the wood; it severs the fibres and gives a cleaner cut.

Steel tape. A 3m (10′) retractable tape is recommended.

Chisel. A 6mm ($\frac{1}{4}$″) is best for making this pot stand.

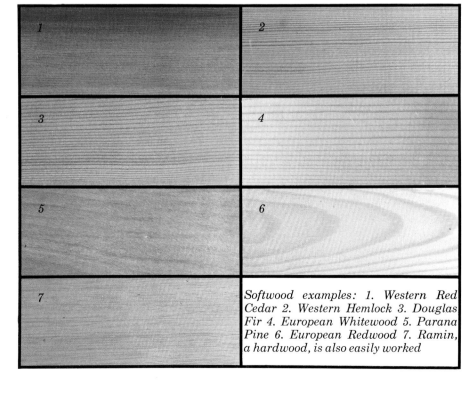

Softwood examples: 1. Western Red Cedar 2. Western Hemlock 3. Douglas Fir 4. European Whitewood 5. Parana Pine 6. European Redwood 7. Ramin, a hardwood, is also easily worked

To make a bench hook

Spread an even layer of wood glue on the face of one strip. Lay this in position and rub to and fro across the

2 stop strips 50mm×25mm (2"×1") of softwood 2cm (5") long

18mm (¾") chipboard or plywood
15cm×30cm (6"×12")

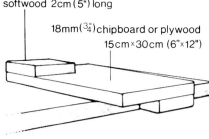

chipboard. As air is squeezed from the joint, the glue forms a strong bond. Repeat for the second side and leave overnight to dry.

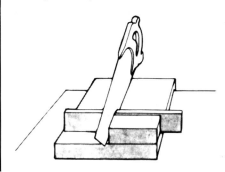

To make the pot stand

This easy-to-make pot stand can be used to protect the table or sideboard from hot casseroles or teapots.

For a pot stand 19cm x 19cm (8" x 8"):

You will need:

A piece of softwood 25mm x 12.5mm (1" x ½"), 2m (6'6") long (allowing for some spare pieces)

Fine glass paper

Optional—9 juniper discs from hobby shops, or slices of ramin dowel, 3cm (1½") diameter; ask a timber merchant to cut them about 5mm (¼") thick

Wood glue

Tools: saw, steel tape, carpenter's square, chisel and trimming knife.

---

1. To 'square off' the wood mark a line about 25mm (1") from the end with the carpenter's square. Place saw on edge of wood and draw it towards you to start the cut. Continue sawing, holding the saw vertically and using even, relaxed strokes.

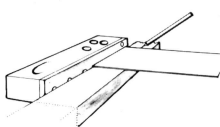

2. Measure off 19cm (8") from the squared off end and mark a line across. Make sure to saw on the outside of this line so the piece will be the full 19cm (8") long—the saw cut is about 2mm ($\frac{1}{10}$") wide.

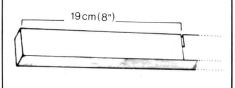

19cm(8")

3. Cut 7 pieces each 19cm (8") long (allowing one spare). On one piece:-
a) Mark off lengths shown along one 12.5mm (½") edge (using the square).
b) Align one of the other pieces along each of these lines and mark along the other side.

3cm 1½" | 6cm 2¼" | 6cm 2¼"

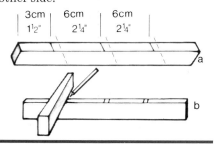

---

4. Holding all the pieces together with ends level, use the square to continue the lines across the other 6 pieces.

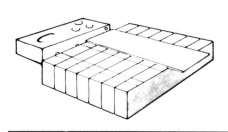

5. Mark 12.5mm (½") down both sides of each piece using a trimming knife. This prepares for a clean cut at stage 6.

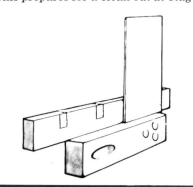

6. On all pieces make 6 cuts on the waste side or inside of each line, so the notch will be the exact width for the cross piece to fit tightly. (Cutting on the line would make notch about 2mm ($\frac{1}{10}$") too big.) First draw in the base lines of notches.

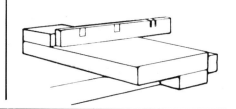

---

7. Put edge of chisel on base line, with sloping face on waste side, and push down. The waste will break off along the grain so, to avoid going over the marked line, work in stages. You might have to turn the wood over to get a square cut.

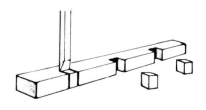

8. Wrap the glass paper around a block of wood and sand each piece. Finish by applying either furniture polish or clear, matt polyurethane.

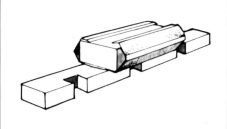

9. Slot the sections together.
10. Glue dowel discs (or juniper) as an alternative finish.

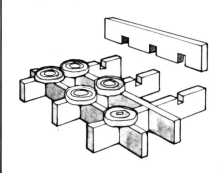

fore starting to saw. Always work from the drawings.

Whereas the pot stand called for enthusiasm and perhaps a little curiosity in beginning, this time perserverance and, as always, a little patience are useful. There are really only one or two steps, which must be repeated over

and over again. But it will offer plenty of sawing practice. It is reassuring to remember that should some saw cuts be a little off and the holes a little too large, a small cover strip nailed to the face side will hide the gaps. Unfortunately it's more difficult to correct errors on the surrounding pieces. The

corner joints, which in this case are the simplest possible, may be difficult to get just right. But this is a learning process and the important thing is that, after a few hours work, you have a useful and attractive spice rack and the satisfaction of knowing that you made it yourself.

Using a hammer

Hammer sizes are determined by the weight of the head. Try to use whichever hammer is available. But if buying one get one that is fairly light and comfortable. Most of the projects involve light nailing—i.e. using panel pins with small heads that can be 'set' into the wood so that they don't show. To hammer a nail use two or three light taps with the hammer while holding the nail. Then use more force, with the fingers out of the way. If the wood surface will be exposed the nail should be driven almost flush with the surface. Don't make dents in the surface by continuing with the hammer if you want to 'hide the nails' below the surface. For this use a nail punch,

or cheat a little and use a larger nail to sink the smaller one.

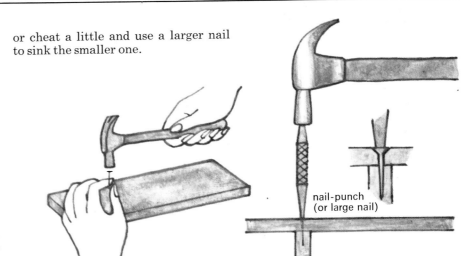

nail-punch (or large nail)

To make the spice rack
You will need:

A piece of softwood 12mm x 75mm ($\frac{1}{2}$"x 3"), 3m (10') long, for grid interior
A piece of softwood 12mm x 100mm ($\frac{1}{2}$"x4"), 2m (6'6") long, for surround
Panel pins (nails) 19mm ($\frac{3}{4}$"), 3 dozen
12mm x 19mm ($\frac{1}{2}$"x$\frac{3}{4}$") beading or softwood strips, 2m (6'6") long (optional)
Fine glasspaper
When buying wood insist on selecting pieces which are straight and free from knots and splits. Very often, if wood is not properly dried or if it hasn't been stored in the correct upright position, it will tend to warp. You can normally spot this but it's useful to sight down

the piece of wood to check that it's fairly straight.
Remember the 12mm x 75mm ($\frac{1}{2}$"x3") or x 100mm (4") dimension is for wood as it is sawn from a large log. The planed size is slightly smaller since a few millimetres are taken off in the planing process. So when planning the sawing remember to measure the actual thickness carefully.

Tools:

Saw
Carpenter's square
Chisel 10mm ($\frac{3}{8}$")
Pencil
Hammer
Steel rule

With the exception of the hammer, all these tools have already been introduced. They are essential equipment and should be found in any tool kit. But it should be emphasized that if one of these is not available it is not absolutely necessary to buy it. Try to improvise. For example, instead of a steel rule an ordinary ruler could be used; and it is possible to substitute a square-cornered piece of cardboard or even a book for a carpenter's square. All that is needed is an accurate 90° angle. Besides, there will be many times when you have misplaced or forgotten a tool. There is, however, no substitute for the saw.

☐ Cut the lengths required. First mark a line about 25mm (1") from the end with a carpenters' square and cut off to start with a 'square' end.
Measure the lengths, mark with carpenters' square, and saw along side of line.

☐ Sand all the pieces using a sanding block. Glass paper comes in various grades from very coarse for rough work to very fine for finishing touches. Sand along the grain, otherwise scratches will show when the piece is finished.

☐ Mark the two 12mm x 75mm ($\frac{1}{2}$"x 3"), 48cm (19") long pieces as shown.
☐ Mark the six 12mm x 75mm ($\frac{1}{2}$"x3"), 30cm (12") long pieces as shown.

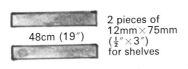

48cm (19")

2 pieces of 12mm×75mm ($\frac{1}{2}$"×3") for shelves

6 pieces of 12mm×75mm ($\frac{1}{2}$"x3") for vertical dividers

30cm (12")

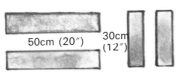

50cm (20")   30cm (12")

4 pieces of 12mm×100mm ($\frac{1}{2}$"×4") for surround 2 pieces 50cm(20") long : 2 pieces 30cm(12") long

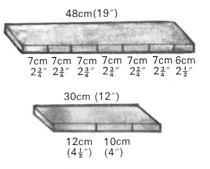

48cm(19")

7cm 7cm 7cm 7cm 7cm 7cm 6cm
2$\frac{3}{4}$" 2$\frac{3}{4}$" 2$\frac{3}{4}$" 2$\frac{3}{4}$" 2$\frac{3}{4}$" 2$\frac{3}{4}$" 2$\frac{1}{2}$"

30cm (12")

12cm   10cm
(4$\frac{1}{2}$")   (4")

☐ When cutting out notches, instead of going through the tedious process of drawing all the lines halfway across every single piece of wood, make a cardboard template as shown.

☐ Place template along marks and mark the notches using a sharp pencil. Mark as shown.

☐ Check that the lines stop at exactly half the width and that the thickness is exactly that of the pieces of wood. Repeat for all six 30cm (12″) pieces and the two 48cm (19″) pieces.

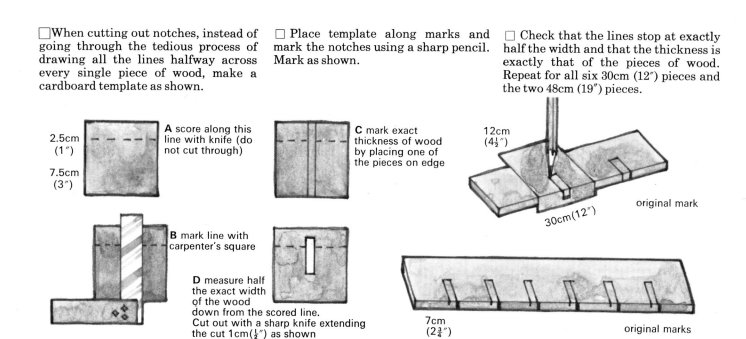

2.5cm (1″)

7.5cm (3″)

A score along this line with knife (do not cut through)

B mark line with carpenter's square

C mark exact thickness of wood by placing one of the pieces on edge

D measure half the exact width of the wood down from the scored line. Cut out with a sharp knife extending the cut 1cm (½″) as shown

12cm (4½″)

30cm(12″)

original mark

7cm (2¾″)

original marks

☐ Sawing on the inside of the line, cut all the pieces as shown.

☐ Using a chisel remove the wood pieces. Place chisel along line and, by pushing gently down, the pieces should come out easily. Square off the cut with the chisel.

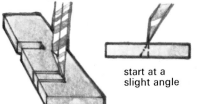

start at a slight angle

☐ After having smoothed all the sawn edges with glass paper, assemble the pieces.

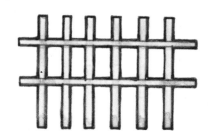

☐ Place the 12mm x 100mm (½″x4″), 30cm (12″) long pieces on the sides, with one edge flush with the back of the interlocking pieces. Sighting from the front, start nailing by tapping lightly with the hammer. The nails must be positioned so that when driven all the way in they will not stick out on the sides. Use two nails for each shelf.

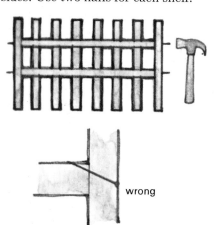

wrong

☐ Now place one of the last two pieces of 12mm x 100mm (½″x4″), 50cm (20″) long, on top and nail along each vertical section.

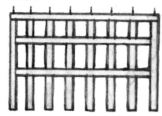

Do the same with bottom piece.
This is a good time to take a little survey and check whether there are any gaps or marks which can be fixed or covered over. You may find that the four corners do not fit perfectly. Unless this is particularly bothersome it is best to leave them and to make sure that you measure more carefully next time. If it's very bad, you can remove the larger piece and cut a bit off if it's too long. If it's too short the only remedy is to make a new piece.

Another possible place where errors can show noticeably is at the junctions of the grid pieces. If the sawcuts were not perfect (which they aren't usually) the only remedy is to cover them up. Strips of wood 12mm x 19mm (½″x¾″), 30cm (12″) long, can be nailed carefully along the front of each of the vertical dividers. Since the strips are about 19mm (¾″) wide they will cover the divider plus the gaps on either side. If there are no bothersome gaps then, of course, the strips are not necessary.

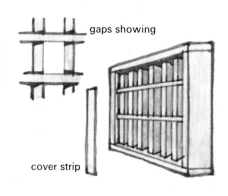

gaps showing

cover strip

The spice rack can either be left without any finish at all or an application of wax or polyurethane wood seal (matt finish) will protect the wood.

If you have any stick-on letters, labels or stencils, these can be used to label each compartment. After applying the labels cover them with a thin coat of clear matt polyurethane so that the letters don't come off when you clean the shelves.

The dimensions of the storage unit can be altered to make it suitable for holding cassettes and books. The addition of a backing board is optional.

Cassette storage unit

Another similar project, shown in the picture, can be built using the same surround dimensions but with fewer internal grid pieces. It is easy to plan this by drawing the pieces and marking the dimensions clearly so that they are easy to follow.

You can add a thin plywood or hardboard backing piece. Your timber merchant will probably cut this accurately if you give the exact dimensions of the overall size of the box. This can be used to glue paper tiles to, either inside or outside. Plan the size of the grid for the particular tile or picture you are planning to use. Then simply nail the backing piece to the back of the assembled unit.

These ideas can be extended to cover a wide range of shelves and storage units depending on how ambitious you are. It would be easy to imagine a whole wall covered with these units, perhaps painted a bright red for the kitchen or white for the living-room. Then not only are the contents displayed but the shelf as well.

The rack can be placed on an existing shelf against a wall or you can fix brackets to the wall on which to rest it.

Wooden boxes in all shapes and sizes

There are many uses for boxes around the home. Smaller boxes are useful for holding trinkets, sewing materials, kitchen utensils and tape cassettes. Others, with handles, can be used as simple 'drawers' for spices and can be made to fit into the compartments of a spice rack. Or use them for storing nails and screws or other hardware. Larger boxes have other uses, such as for storing blankets and pillows under

the bed, for children's toys or even as window boxes to put plants in.

The construction of a box is very simple; it has four sides, a bottom and sometimes a top or lid. The nice thing is that this basic structure doesn't change—no matter how large the box is. So, a jewelry box is made with the same basic construction as a box for toys or tools. The main difference is in the strength of the box. For a small box it is enough to nail the sides together at the corners, whereas for a large, heavy box some metal brackets and screws will be required.

Since they are so easy to make, boxes are particularly useful and rewarding projects that can be finished in an afternoon or two. A small box with a hinged lid can be adapted to hold various things and it can also be finished according to your taste. It can be dressed in an attractive fabric with a similar lining on the inside.

There are many possibilities for boxes that you can adapt to your own needs. You may have a sofa or a window seat with space underneath for a few storage boxes. It's easy to measure the height and depth and then to draw up the size of box, or boxes you need. You can buy handles in hardware stores that are very easy to attach.

Plywood

Plywood is made of layers of veneer glued together. The layers are glued together with the grain of each successive layer running at cross angles to one another. This strengthens the plywood and, in the thicker sizes prevents it from shrinking and splitting.

Plywood varies in thickness from 3mm ($\frac{1}{8}$") to 6mm ($\frac{1}{4}$") and multi-ply from 8mm ($\frac{5}{16}$") to 25mm (1").

It can be bought with various surface finishes such as pine, birch and ash. Hardwood veneer is also used for a surface finish, making it a very useful and inexpensive alternative for covering large areas where a good finish is required.

To make a small box

This box, when completed, measures 20cm x 17cm (8"x7"), height 8cm (3"). Depending on the finish, you can use it for trinkets, cosmetics or sewing materials. If you use it for jewelry you can line the inside with felt or velvet or adhesive-backed plush; for sewing materials you can sub-divide the box in the same way as the shelf units.

By cutting out the wood where the hinges are placed, the lid fits flat on the box. A notch cut in the front forms a recess for a finger to lift the lid.

The box can be completed in a number of ways; it can be stained or polished and the inside can be lined with felt.

You will need:
Tools
Hammer.
Saw.
Screwdriver.
Carpenter's square.
Pencil.
Ruler or tape measure.
Chisel.
Nail punch.
Trimming knife (optional).
Materials
Softwood, 8cm x 12mm (3"x$\frac{1}{2}$"), 76cm (30") long.
Plywood, 20cm x 36cm (8"x15"), 6mm ($\frac{1}{4}$") thick—birch plywood is ideal but any small offcut will do.
Panel pins, 2.5cm (1"), about 24.
Brass hinges, 2 small ones with 6mm ($\frac{1}{4}$") screws.
Medium and fine glasspaper.
Wood glue.

1. From the softwood mark and cut 2 pieces 20cm (8") long and 2 pieces 15cm (6") long.
Sand the rough ends lightly.

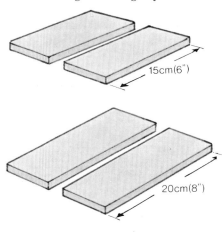

To make a notch (to allow you to get your fingers under the lid to open it)
2. Take one of the 20cm (8") pieces, mark as shown and make a small indentation with the chisel. To do this lay the piece flat, and, putting a little pressure on the chisel, score along two sides with a trimming knife, then slice off the wood as shown. You can omit this if it's too difficult.

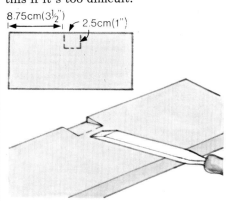

To nail the sides together
3. Starting with a 20cm (8") side put the nails in halfway while the piece of wood is flat on the work surface.
Then complete nailing, as shown, after you have put some glue on the surfaces —ie one nail for every corner.
4. Turn the box over and nail on the 3rd and 4th pieces.

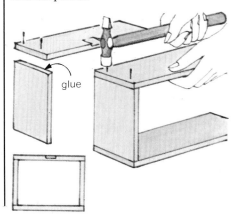

To make the base and lid
5. Hold the box on the plywood so that the sides meet the ends of the box. Mark off as shown and saw off.

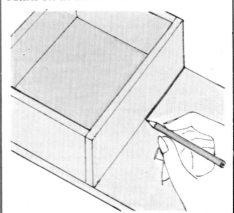

6. Use this piece of plywood to mark one additional piece then saw off to the same size.

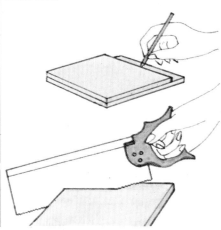

7. Tap 4 nails part of the way into the plywood for the base. Put a small amount of glue on the 4 bottom edges of the box. Put the plywood piece on to the glued edges of the box. Make sure that it is placed correctly as you drive in the nails. Put in another 6 or 8 nails.

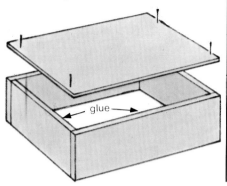

To put the hinges on

8. Start with the lid. Measure 4cm (1½") in from the ends along one 20cm (8") edge and mark a line to use as a guide when attaching the hinges. Place the hinge on the inside of this line and mark the outline.

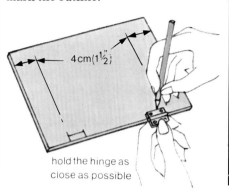

4cm(1½")

hold the hinge as close as possible

9. Using the chisel, make a recess for the hinge. The easiest way is to score marks along the 3 sides to the depth of the hinge thickness and then remove the wood from the side.

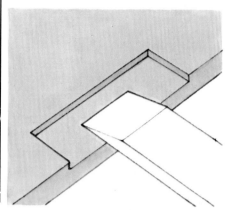

10. Insert the hinge and mark the holes for the screws. Using a nail punch, punch a small hole in the centre of each mark.

11. Using the small brass screws, screw the hinge to the lid. Repeat for the other hinge.

12. Place the lid on the box and mark lines along the sides of the hinges. Score these lines. (Make sure that the lid is held flush all round.)

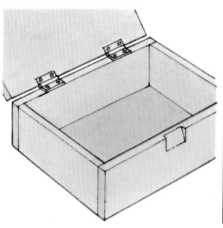

13. Using the chisel, remove the wood where the hinges fit. The notch should be very shallow—only as deep as the thickness of one leaf of the hinge.

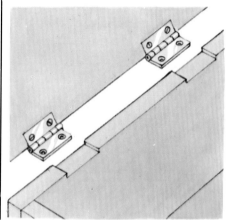

14. Holding the lid in position, mark the screw-holes, then punch small holes and screw the lid to the box.

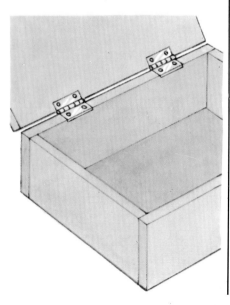

15. Sand the box using first the medium glasspaper, then the fine glasspaper. You can round the edges a little to give the box a softer appearance.

16. If you want to paint the box, fill the cracks along the edges with a cellulose filler, let it dry and sand it smooth.
The box can be left natural and covered with a coat of clear, matt polyurethane or designs and patterns can be painted on top of a base colour.

Instead of making a finger notch on the front of the box, a brass hook and eye can be used. Designer A. Martensson.

Alternative designs

Stacking boxes can be painted bright colours and stick-on letters or numbers can be used to decorate them.
Make the sides, say, 23cm (9″) deep and nail on a bottom to each box.
Underneath, at each corner, nail and glue a small block of plywood, positioned to miss the sides of the box below. This will hold the stacked boxes in position.
Only the top box has a lid. The lid is not hinged as before but is made from 2 pieces of plywood—one the same size as the bottom and the other to fit inside the box. Glue the 2 pieces together.

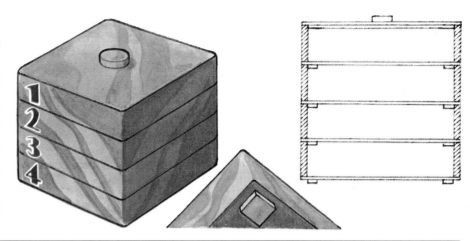

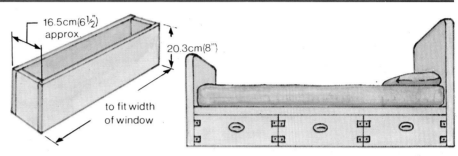

Window box. Make the sides from plywood at least 12mm (½″) thick and use screws instead of nails to put it together. Drill small holes in the bottom for drainage.

Boxes under the bed. Use materials similar to those for the window box and attach metal brackets to the corners. Bought handles are easy to screw on.

Boxes for drawers. Make handles from blocks of wood or pieces of dowel and attach by screwing in from the back. Alternatively, bought handles can be screwed on from the front.

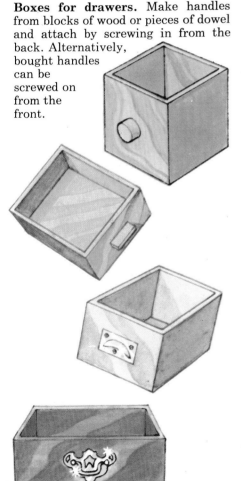

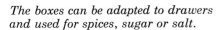

The boxes can be adapted to drawers and used for spices, sugar or salt.

Dowelling: round pegs in circular holes

Dowels

A dowel is a rod-like piece of wood with a round cross-section. Dowels are referred to by their diameter and are available in various sizes up to 2.5cm (1″).

One reason for the versatility of dowels is that they are so easy to join to other pieces of wood—all you need is a drilled hole the same diameter as the dowel. It's much easier to make a round hole with a drill than to make a square hole, which requires chisels, mallets and accurate marking.

Before the mass production of nails and screws, hand-made dowels or 'pegs' were often used to secure the join between two pieces of wood—this is often seen in the roofing structure of old barns.

Dowels can be used in many ways—to make struts or dividers as in plate or record racks; to make racks for shoes, towels; to make shelves for hats or phone books, or to make legs and supports for shelves.

In the towel rack illustrated the dowels are exposed and are an intrinsic feature of the design. To connect them to the side pieces requires a simple operation of drilling a hole and pushing the dowels in, with a drop of glue to hold them in position.

You can use a power tool to do the work, but hand tools are more satisfying to use for smaller projects and have the advantage of being able to make larger holes for larger dowels.

To make the towel rack

This project involves simple, versatile techniques—drilling and using dowels. Small pieces of dowel are used to 'lock' the ends of the rack in position. It is an awkward operation drilling the holes for the small dowels so you can leave them out and simply glue and nail the side pieces in position if you prefer.

You will need:

Softwood 38cm x 15cm (15″x6″), 2.5cm (1″) thick.

Dowel 2.5cm (1″) diameter and 127cm (50″) long.

Dowel 6mm ($\frac{1}{4}$″) diameter and 48cm (19″) long (optional) or 4 panel pins 3cm ($1\frac{1}{4}$″) long.

Fine grade glasspaper.

Wood glue.

2 brass strips 6cm ($2\frac{1}{4}$″) long with 4 holes in each strip and screws for attaching the rack to the wall.

You may not be able to buy the wood and dowel to the exact lengths given, but any pieces left over are always useful for making something else. Make sure that the dowels you use are the same size as the drill bits.

This towel rail is made by drilling and inserting pieces of dowel through the holes. Designed by Alf Martensson.

Tool box

Drills, braces, drill bits

The bit is the part that actually cuts the wood. It is fitted into either a brace or hand drill. The large diameter auger bits—from 6mm ($\frac{1}{4}$") to 25mm (1") diameter—are usually used with a brace and the smaller twist drill bits with a hand drill.

The hand drill is for smaller, lighter work whereas, with the brace, you can drill holes up to 75mm (3") in diameter using special expansion bits.

If you do not have access to a brace and have to buy one, then the rachet type is recommended. A brace and a hand drill are essential to a tool kit.

The bit fits into the jaws of the drill. The jaws open or close with the turning of the chuck. When the jaws are open insert the bit and tighten up well.

To drill a hole mark the centre of the hole with a pencil and, using either a nail or nail punch, make a small hole to start the drilling. This prevents the bit from slipping and ensures that the hole will be exactly where you want it. Place the point of the bit into this hole and turn the handle slowly. Make sure that you hold the drill at 90° to the piece of wood—the drill must be in this position throughout the operation.

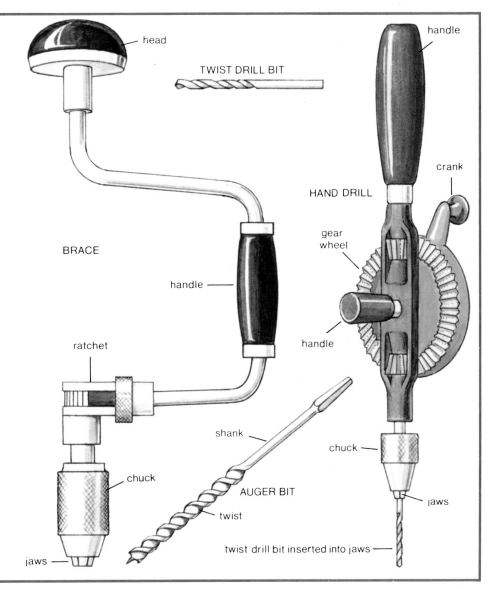

Tools

Brace with 2.5cm (1") bit.
Hand drill with 6mm ($\frac{1}{4}$") bit—you will only need this if you are using the 6mm ($\frac{1}{4}$") dowel.
Saw, nail-punch, hammer, carpenter's square, G–clamp or vice.

1. Using the carpenter's square, square the short end of the softwood about 2cm ($\frac{3}{4}$") from the end. Cut off on the waste side.

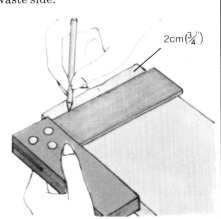

2. Mark off lengths and cut as shown.
3. Draw diagonals as shown and make a mark 5cm (2") from each corner and punch a small hole.

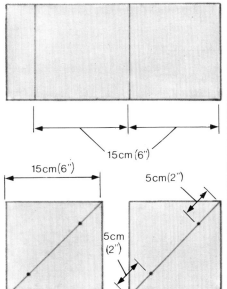

4. Using the brace with 2.5cm (1") bit, drill a hole on each mark. When the bit pierces through the bottom, turn the wood over and complete the hole from this side.
5. Sand both pieces until smooth. You can round the ends slightly to improve the appearance.

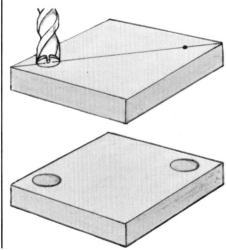

6. Cut 2 pieces of dowel 61cm (24") long from the 2.5cm (1") dowel.

61cm(24")

7. If you are not using the 6mm (¼") dowel insert the 2 pieces of dowel through the holes in the softwood sides and let 2.5cm (1") protrude from the ends. Secure the dowels with 3cm (1¼") panel pins.

8. To assemble the rack using the 6mm (¼") dowel cut 8 pieces 5.5cm (2¼") long.

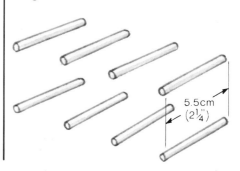

5.5cm (2¼")

9. At 2cm (¾") from each end of the two 2.5cm (1") dowels make a mark as shown. Make another mark 3.2cm (1¼") inside each of these making 8 in all. Punch a small hole at each of the marks
10. Secure the dowel and drill a hole with the 6mm (¼") bit on each of the 8 marks. Make sure to d.ill the hole through the thickest part of the dowel.

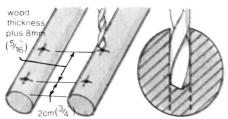

wood thickness plus 8mm (⁵⁄₁₆")

2cm(¾")

11. Sand all the ends smooth and assemble as shown using a bit of wood glue if necessary. Paint or stain the rack as required.

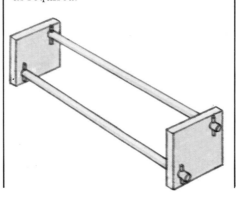

12. Attach the rack to the wall using brass strips as shown.

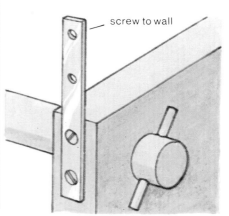

screw to wall

Alternative ideas

This rack can be made to hold spoons used for cooking. You can alter the size to suit metal or wooden spoons, in fact you can make it to hold most of your cooking utensils, including a soup ladle. To support the rack you can screw hooks into the top and suspend it from a shelf.

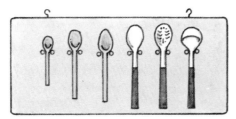

An alternative to the spoon rack is a cutlery tray. Make it to fit into an existing drawer and use it to keep knives, forks etc stacked together.

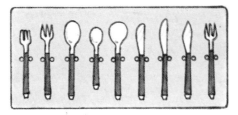

A toast rack is attractive and easy to make.
This type of rack can also be made on a larger scale to hold long-playing records.

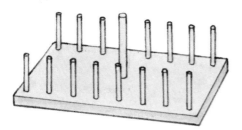

A thick dowel used as a curtain rod for heavy curtains is attractive without a pelmet.

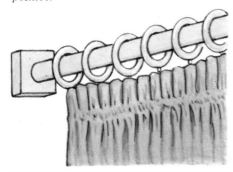

Left. Plate rack: to assemble base drill holes near ends of both main pieces making sure they do not coincide with one of the upright pieces of dowel.

There is plenty of drilling practice in making this knife rack. A saw cut in the larger dowel secures the blade.

A hat rack is always useful and you can put it up somewhere convenient and out of the way. You can expand it by using a long, flat piece of wood with dowels interspersed at regular intervals from which to hang coats. You could also make a rack to run the length of a wardrobe to keep shoes tidy.

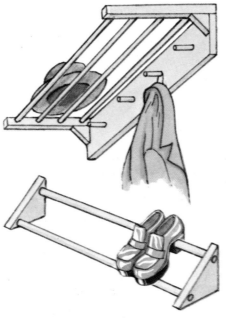

This gate is very useful to prevent children from falling downstairs or out of windows.

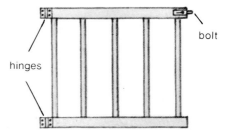

An egg rack is always useful and you can easily make it to hold more than six eggs. This particular rack can be stacked so that you can put any number together without damaging the eggs. Make the dowel supports long enough to prevent the eggs from being crushed. Do not push the dowels all the way through the wood but leave about 6mm ($\frac{1}{4}''$) from the top to hold another rack secure when you stack them.

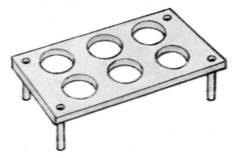

Making and installing your own shelves

One of the reasons for the popularity of carpentry today is that it is so practical. Everyone has his or her own reasons for enjoying making things, but for most it is the satisfaction of having made something useful and saving money at the same time.

Every home needs shelves for storage space—few kitchens have sufficient shelving, in the living room shelves are needed for books and records and in the bedroom and bathroom shelves have a variety of uses.

It takes very little skill and time to put up a shelf and there are several ways of doing it, so choose the most appropriate, then add a little extra imagination and craftsmanship to the detail and finish.

Measuring. To find the length of board you will need, measure accurately and make sure the tape is in a horizontal position. If you are building a number of shelves against a wall measure the width at the top and at the bottom of the wall as it could vary, in which case you must adjust the length of the boards accordingly.

Wall-fixed or free-standing shelves

Shelves supported on walls involve drilling a hole in the wall for a wall plug to take the screw. It is easy to

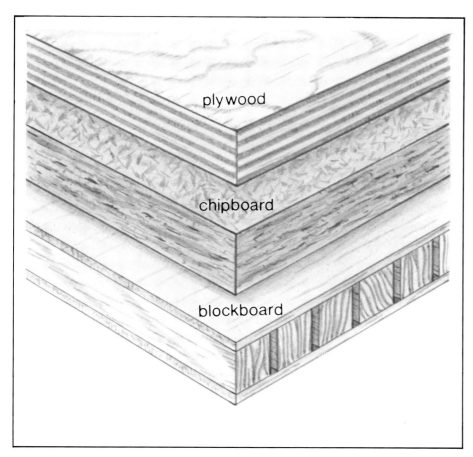

Man-made boards are available in various thicknesses and surface finishes.

put in a wall plug, especially if you have an electric drill.

Alternatively, you can build free-standing shelving. The method shown here does not involve complicated joinery and is quick and easy.

Shelving boards

Softwood. The easiest material to use is ordinary softwood boards about 2cm ($\frac{3}{4}''$) thick. The width and length depend on your particular requirements but boards about 22cm–26cm (9''–10'') wide are ideal for most books. Measure the length of the individual shelves and calculate the total length of the board required.

You can have the boards cut to the length you require when buying them. If you have suitable boards that need cutting to size, measure and mark them. Use a carpenter's square to get a straight end and saw off the excess.

Since timber is cut to fixed lengths discuss your requirements with the timber merchant who will then cut from existing boards the exact lengths you want for your shelves.

Useful and economical substitutes for softwood board for shelves are man-made boards.

An alcove lends itself to shelving—it provides storage space without projecting into the room. In this system cleats are used for supports.

Man-made boards have advantages over softwood boards in that they can be bought in almost any size and are not limited in width as is timber. Also, man-made boards will not warp if properly and adequately supported.

The boards vary in strength, appearance and cost. The only problem with these boards is that cut ends are not attractive and need to be finished neatly. It does not matter if the ends are out of sight, but if they show they should be covered with a facing strip—any strip of wood or veneer will do.

Plywood is a flat board made of veneers in layers and at cross grain. The number of layers is always odd to prevent the board from warping. The boards are available in various finishes, including a hardwood surface or a plastic laminate. Thickness varies from 8mm ($\frac{1}{3}''$) to 25mm (1'').

Plywood is strong enough for most shelving, except where a very heavy object, such as a television set, will be resting on it.

Chipboard or particle board is made of wood chips which are pressed and glued together. The glue content in the board acts as an abrasive so any tools used to cut the board will become blunt more quickly than when cutting wood. However, it is inexpensive and can be used for shelving if supported at regular intervals.

The edges are not very strong so, to

prevent them from chipping away, nail a thin strip of wood to the edges for protection.

Chipboard is also available with a plastic or hardwood finish which improves the appearance and strengthens the board. Thickness of chipboard varies between 3.2mm ($\frac{1}{8}''$) and 50mm (2''). For shelving use board between 13mm ($\frac{1}{2}''$) and 25mm (1)'' thick. It's excellent for book shelves.

Blockboard is a thick, strong board made of wood strips, 19mm–25mm ($\frac{3}{4}''$–1'') thick, glued together between veneers of solid wood. It is much stronger than chipboard and is ideal for use as heavy duty shelving where long, narrow strips of board have to bear a heavy load. The grain must run along the length of the shelf.

A veneer or strip of wood is essential to the edges of blockboard as the spaces between the interior blocks are rather unsightly.

Wall shelves

To attach a shelf to the wall you will need to drill a hole and insert a wall plug to receive the screw.

To drill a hole in the wall. Mark the location of the hole and use a masonry drill bit (a No.10 bit for a No.10 plug) and drill to the depth that the screw will penetrate the wall.

Slide wall plug into hole.

Put the screw through whatever you are attaching to the wall and screw into centre of plug until it won't go any further.

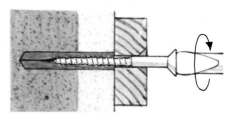

The screw is turned into the plug.

Supporting the shelves. There are several methods of supporting shelves. If the shelves are to fit into an alcove or a recess the easiest way to support them is to use a strip of wood at both ends—called a cleat.

You could also use metal strips, as for adjustable shelving, or L-shaped brackets in wood or metal. If the shelves do not fit into an alcove you can use any method except the cleat supports.

You will need:

Tools

A drill—an electric drill is best but you can use a hand drill and work a bit harder.

A masonry drill bit for No.10 plugs.

Medium sized screwdriver.

Spirit level.

Saw.

Trimming knife—optional.

Shelf brackets. There are many types of brackets available, from elaborate ones to the simple modern L-brackets (fig.1). These screw into the wall and also have one or two holes for screws that hold the shelf down securely.

To put up a wall shelf hold one bracket in position against the wall. Mark the holes with a pencil.

Drill holes and insert wall plug.

Attach bracket to wall with screws.

Hold shelf with one end resting on the bracket. Place the spirit level on the shelf, check that it is level and mark the holes for the other bracket.

Drill the holes, insert the plugs and screw the bracket to the wall.

Screw the shelf, from the underside, to the brackets with screws that will not go all the way through the shelf.

Metal brackets support this shelving.

Tool box

Tools and hardware

Screws and Plugs. There are various types of screws—some have round heads, some flat, some are made of steel and others of brass. In woodwork flat-headed screws are usually used. Use ordinary steel screws or, if the heads show and you want them to look nicer, use brass screws.

You order screws by the length and the diameter. The diameter is indicated in numbers.

The higher the number the larger the screw.

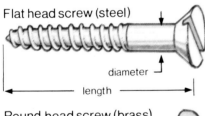

Flat head screw (steel)

diameter

length

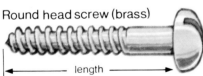

Round head screw (brass)

length

If you try to drill a hole into a brick wall and then put a screw into it, the screw will pull out easily because it doesn't 'bite' into the masonry the way it does into wood. Therefore, drill a hole slightly larger than the screw and fill the hole with a special wall plug and then turn the screw into the plug. The screw is held secure because it forces the plug very tightly against the sides of the hole.

There are various types of wall plugs available, from the old-fashioned fibre plugs to the newer plastic ones. All are equally adequate.

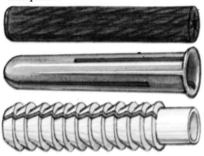

Each screw size is used together with one particular size of wall plug. Thus a No.10 screw is used with a No.10 plug. The plugs can be bought in rods and cut to the required lengths with a trimming knife or they can be bought to match the screws being used.

Use a screwdriver that fits the groove on the screw.

Spirit level. A level will tell you just that—when things are level. The bubble will be centred between the little lines when it is exactly level. So rest the level on the shelf and raise or lower one end until it is level. A spirit level is inexpensive and available from hardware stores.

Cover strip. An attractive way to cover the shelves so that the cleats do not show is to nail strips to the front of the shelves (fig.3). You can buy mahogany strips and nail them with panel pins to the shelves. Set the nails with a nail punch.

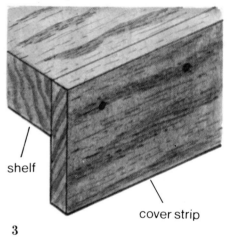

shelf

cover strip

3

Free-standing shelves

You will need:

Hammer, saw.

Tape measure or ruler.

Glue.

A sheet of 3mm ($\frac{1}{8}$") hardboard to nail to the back of the bookcase.

The main advantage of free-standing shelves (fig.5a) is that they can be moved from one room to another or from one home to another. So if, for whatever reason, you can't drill into the walls or you don't have a drill then the self-supporting shelves are ideal.

Use timber 2cm ($\frac{3}{4}$") thick for the shelves and the vertical supports. There are several ways of attaching the shelves to the upright sides, the quickest being to nail and glue a cleat horizontally to the sides.

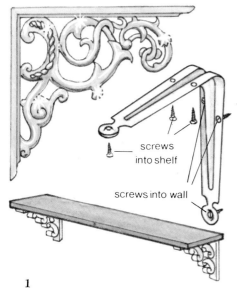

Shelves in an alcove. These are supported at either end by a cleat (a strip of wood) which is attached to the wall with screws (fig.2). Cleats can be cut from any softwood 50mm x 25mm (2″x1″). The length should not be more than the width of the shelf.

Drill holes for wall plugs and attach one cleat.

Hold up shelf with spirit level on it and mark holes for the other cleat.

The shelf can be secured by nailing panel pins through the shelf into the cleats.

1

2

Adjustable shelves. You can buy these shelf systems consisting of three parts: vertical supports, brackets, shelves (fig.4).

The vertical supports are so made that any number of brackets can move up or down once the supports have been attached to the wall. The brackets vary in size—short brackets to hold a narrow shelf or longer ones to hold wider and heavier shelving.

There are various brands of adjustable shelving available but they all work on the same principle and are installed similarly. The main difference is in appearance and the weight that they can support. The more expensive types are for heavy duty shelving.

If you decide on this type of shelving discuss the shelving board and the length of the shelves with the shop-keeper who will recommend a suitable

metal support and bracket.

For simplicity and neat appearance these shelves are good value and can be finished in any way you wish.

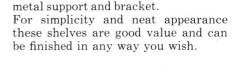

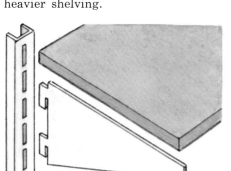

4

If you wish to hide the cleats, add a cover strip to the uprights (fig. 5b).

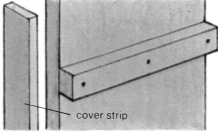

cover strip

5b

The only problem is that these shelves will topple sideways unless you nail a sheet of hardboard 3mm ($\frac{1}{8}$″) thick to the back, using 2cm ($\frac{3}{4}$″) panel pins (fig.5c).

You can paint the front of the hard-

board backing so that it provides a colourful backing to the shelves or cover it with plywood if you want a wood finish to show.

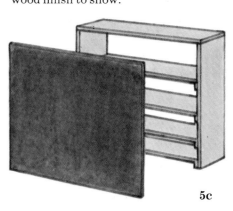

5a

5c

The varieties and the uses of hardwood

The word 'hardwood' does not necessarily mean that a wood is hard. For example balsa wood, which is very soft, is a hardwood. Generally, broad-leaved trees come under this category. The term 'softwood' covers all coniferous or conebearing trees having pointed leaves, such as pine, fir and spruce. Hardwood and softwood therefore denote the two main botanical families into which timber types are divided.

Softwood, which is generally blonde, is traditionally associated with Scandinavian furniture but in other countries hardwoods are preferred—most antique furniture was made from hardwood. Hardwoods such as oak, mahogany and beech are widely used for furniture because they are attractive, strong and pleasing to work with.

World trade in timber has developed to such an extent that it is possible to buy furniture made from any chosen timber. People generally buy hardwood furniture because, with the exception of balsa wood, hardwoods are harder than softwoods, tend to be stronger and heavier, and can be given a variety of finishes. The main attraction of hardwood is the variety of colour and grain patterns that are available. Unfortunately, hardwood has also become expensive and frequently modern furniture is made from man-made board which has been covered with a hardwood veneer. This makes the furniture economical while still retaining the solid appearance and finish of a hardwood. Some of the more decorative hardwoods such as rosewood and walnut are not readily available but it is usually possible to obtain them in the form of veneers.

The hardwoods illustrated will give you some idea of the different timbers. You will not necessarily be able to buy them from your local timber yard. It is impossible for a timber yard to stock such a wide range and, of course, it also depends on the availability of the different types of tree.

About hardwoods

The process that begins with a tree in a tropical forest and ends with a plank in a workshop is a lengthy one.

In tropical conditions such as are found in West Africa and Malaysia trees grow quickly and, because they grow all year round, they do not have the marks or rings showing annual growth which distinguish most woods from cooler climates.

Converting logs

Once cut, logs are converted into planks. The logs are generally cut in one of two ways depending on the kind of tree and the use to which the wood will be put.

The simplest, cheapest and most common way, is the slab method (fig.1) where a gigantic saw cuts the log into planks.

The other way is known as quarter sawing (fig.2). It is used to produce attractive surface figuring and with sapele it produces a striped effect which distinguishes it from most other African timbers. A quarter-sawn plank will

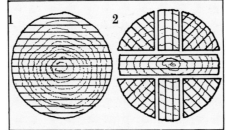

1. Slab method 2. Quarter sawing.

keep flatter than a plank cut in slabs.
Seasoning. The planks must be seasoned before they are used otherwise the timber will shrink and warp. The cut logs contain a lot of moisture which must be seasoned or dried out. This is done after converting the logs into planks. The planks are laid out in a dry atmosphere—large kilns or ovens are used in countries with a high rainfall. Seasoning planks in a kiln takes about two weeks.

Colours. The most readily available hardwoods can be classified into three categories according to their colour:
Blonde or straw coloured: ash, oak, beech, ramin, maple and obeche.
Red: utile, sapele, keruing and meranti. The red woods are very similar in appearance and timber merchants often sell them under the general label of mahogany. Try to find out exactly what you are buying as each timber behaves differently especially when joined or finished.
Brown: iroko, afrormosia, teak and elm (light brown). Brown hardwoods are often confused with teak which is generally better known than the others. As for the red hardwoods, try to ascertain exactly what you buy.

Buying hardwood.
You should be able to select a suitable hardwood from a timber yard, ie if you cannot get one of your choice there should be one of a similar colour or grain—if this is more important (the colour can always be changed with wood stain).

Hardwood is sold in various sizes, the timber will be sawn but not planed, ie it will have a rough surface and the overall size will be decreased slightly once the timber is planed to a smooth surface. When you buy sawn timber ask the timber merchant to plane it down for you. Make it quite clear that the measurements you need are for planed timber otherwise the sawn timber once planed might be too small for your purpose. The timber is always referred to by its cross-section and then the length, for example 25mm x 50mm (1"x2"), 1m (1yd) long.

Now, understanding more about hardwoods you can make any of the projects discussed previously, in a much greater choice of materials. Thus, for example, a jewelry box or a shelf unit would both be very attractive made in hardwood and would also give you the opportunity to finish the surface with wax or a matt polyurethane varnish to show the hardwood at its best—the choice of finish is optional.

5   6   7   8

2	**3**	**4**

Timber	Colour	Origin	Characteristics	Uses
ASH 1	Yellowish white	Europe Canada	Long grain and elastic.	Tool handles and sports goods.
OBECHE 2	Pale yellow	West Africa	Soft even texture. Light in weight. Nails, screws, stains and polishes well.	Kitchen cabinets and 'white-wood' furniture.
RAMIN 3	Oatmeal	Malaysia	Strong close grain.	Mouldings, picture framing, whitewood furniture framework.
BEECH 4	Cream or light pink	Europe	Close grained and hard. Excellent for bending.	The most widely used timber in the furniture industry.
DARK RED MERANTI 5	Dark red-brown	Malaysia, Sarawak, Borneo	Uniform grain. Pin holes in some boards.	General purpose hardwood cut for plywood veneers.
SAPELE 6	Red	East and West Africa	Striped effect on some boards. Uneven grain.	Furniture and drawers. Best veneers seen on wardrobes etc.
KERUING 7	Red	Malaysia	Can be sticky with resin. Moderately durable.	Structural work on housing and exterior joinery.
UTILE 8	Dark red	West Africa	Easier to work than Sapele.	'Mahogany' type furniture construction.
OAK 9	Straw to light brown	Europe, Japan Canada, Australia	Avoid contact with iron, eg steel screws which stain. Strong and reliable.	Used for shopfittings, desks etc. Best wood for facing veneers.
IROKO 10	Light to dark brown	West Africa	High resistance to decay and strong.	Ideal worktop material.
AFRORMOSIA 11	Honey to brown	West Africa	High resistance to decay.	Dining-room furniture. Show parts of upholstered suites.
TEAK 12	Brown, sometimes light in colour	Burma, India	Fire resistant, strong and versatile.	High-class joinery and general carpentry.
ELM (not illustrated)	Light brown	Europe	Long lasting and very strong.	Chair seats, wood carving and coffins.

10	**11**	**12**

Techniques of planing and joinery

We have the pleasure of seeing and feeling the natural beauty of hardwoods every day and can learn to recognize a wide variety of different woods by their distinctive colours and grain patterns. And because they are strong we can appreciate their usefulness. However, it is only through cutting and working with hardwoods that one appreciates their characteristics.

It is usual to buy hardwood which has been machine planed on both sides (PBS). Do remember to specify PBS when buying hardwood and ask the machinist to plane one or both edges as well. Despite the fact that the timber merchant will plane the timber for you, you might still need to trim it yourself, for example, if you are constructing joints you need to work very accurately to get good results. So, although the timber has a smooth surface you might still have to trim it yourself for a specific purpose.

To work accurately use a carpenter's square to check that one edge is square, ie at right angles to the side (fig.1).

Use the marking gauge against this edge to mark the exact width that you want the wood to be. This is most important when two pieces of wood need to be exactly the same width.

1. *Before trimming a piece of wood check that the edge is square.*

Tool box

Marking gauge
This simple wooden tool scribes (scratches) a line along the grain parallel to the edge of or side of a piece of wood. It is used when a piece of timber has to be trimmed to a particular width or thickness.

The marking gauge consists of a wooden shaft with an adjustable crosspiece sliding up and down it. At one end of the shaft there is a metal spike.

The crosspiece is set to the required distance from the spike. The tool is then moved along the side or edge of the wood. The metal spike will mark a straight line with a constant distance from the side or edge as the crosspiece keeps it in position. Always slide the marking gauge against the grain, so that the slope of the grain holds it in position.

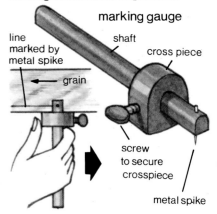

marking gauge

line marked by metal spike — shaft — cross piece — grain — screw to secure crosspiece — metal spike

Planes
A plane is used to smooth the surface of a piece of wood, or to trim it down to a required size leaving a smooth surface.

There is a variety of planes available, each having a specific function.

A **bench plane** is available in three lengths. The short one is a smoothing plane for smoothing already flat timber. The medium length is a jack plane and is used for shaping rough wood. The long plane is a trying plane for creating an accurate flat surface.

A **block plane** cuts very cleanly and is only used to cut end grain.

All the above planes cut with a blade referred to as a plane iron, which must be sharpened occasionally.

If you are only doing the occasional bit of carpentry you will not want to buy all the special purpose planes available.

Replaceable blades
A useful plane is one that has replaceable blades, ie once the cutting edge is blunt the blade is thrown away and a new one inserted—like a razor blade. The blades are available with a straight edge or a curved edge which does make the plane more versatile.

A straight edged blade is used to trim and smooth edges where only a small amount of timber has to be removed. If more than 3mm (⅛″) of timber has to be removed a carpenter will use a jack plane, but a blade with a curved edge will do exactly the same thing. The straight edged blade will remove only a small bit of wood on each stroke. The curved blade will speed things up.

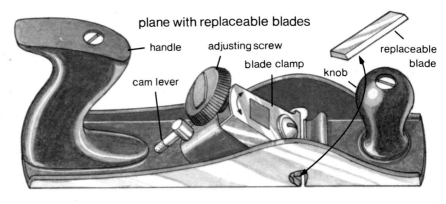

plane with replaceable blades

handle — adjusting screw — replaceable blade — blade clamp — knob — cam lever

The adjusting screw moves the blade further out of the plane to increase the depth of the cut.

The blade clamp and the adjusting screw hold the blade parallel to the flat bottom surface of the plane. This is very important so always check the blade before planing.

The cam lever releases the blade.

The clamping screw should not be too tight otherwise any adjustment to the blade will be difficult.

Planing

Hold the wood in a vice or clamp, protecting the wood surface if necessary with a piece of waste wood.

Trim the length of the timber first and make sure that it is at right angles to the sides.

Trimming to length

A piece of timber might be a fraction too long or have a rough end (end grain) which you want to smooth. You can use a plane to do the job but it must be done carefully. Practise on a piece of waste wood first.

Ideally you need a block plane. If you are using a plane with a replaceable blade make sure that the blade is sharp, use a straight edged blade, and set it as fine as possible, that is to remove a very thin bit of wood.

The problem with planing end grain is that once the blade reaches the end of the piece of timber it can rip and splinter the end of the wood. To avoid this hold the timber in a vice and trim to the marked line working towards the centre from both edges (fig.2). In other words you will be planing at a slight angle, working towards the centre and never going across the entire length of the timber. Work in stages, a few strokes from either edge, then work towards the centre until the edge is straight.

Working along the grain

Keep the plane level—not an easy thing to do when the experience is new —and make certain that you do not plane below the marked line.

Avoid rounding the edge on a long length of timber. Put more pressure on the front of the plane (the round knob) at the beginning of the stroke, and at the end, apply more pressure at the back (handle).

Before you get down to the marked line use the carpenter's square to check that the side or edge being planed is at 90° to the adjoining side. Make any adjustment necessary and plane down to the marked line.

Always work in the direction of the grain (fig.3) If you plane against the grain you will end up with a heavily pitted surface which is difficult to finish well.

Planing large flat surfaces

The quality of machine planing can vary enormously and if a timber merchant has used sharp cutters, finely set, the timber surface should be good. If it has been done carelessly the surface will not be very good so it is always wise to check the surface when buying timber.

A well planed surface will only need a bit of fine grade glasspaper along its grain to finish it before polishing.

If the timber surface is pitted or rough and you want to smooth it, fit a new straight edged blade in the plane. Make

sure it is parallel to the flat surface of the plane and that it is set as finely as possible. Test it on a piece of waste wood.

Check the direction of the grain by looking at the edge of the piece of wood (fig.4). Plane in the direction of the grain with firm even strokes. If you plane against the grain you will roughen the surface.

If a piece of timber is difficult to smooth, perhaps because of awkward

The plane is held as shown and pushed with firm, even strokes.

grain or bad handling, you can use a proprietary wood filler at this stage to improve the surface. Do this carefully and follow the manufacturer's instructions. You can then finish it with a high gloss polyurethane varnish. If you want a matt finish the surface of the wood must be good without the use of a wood filler.

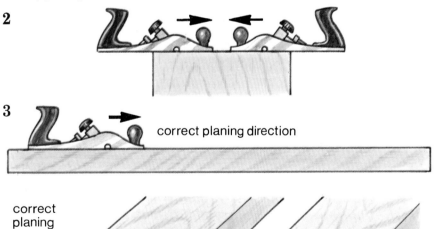

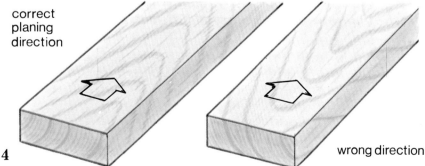

2. *Two ways of planing end grain to avoid breaking and splintering the ends.*
3. *Grain along edge shows planing direction.* **4.** *Grain on facing surface.*

Simple joints

Hardwood joints

You might not need to, or want to, cut wood for joints, but it is good to know the basic ones so you will have some idea of how they are used to make up the furniture that we use every day. You will also have some idea of what is involved should you want to repair a piece of furniture which has come undone at a joint and requires a bit of glue to secure it.

The butt joint (fig.5) is the simplest of all joints. It may be made straight, two pieces edge to edge, or at right-angles, and needs nails, glue or screws to hold it together.

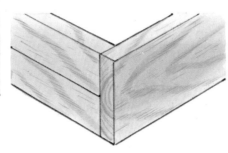

A dowelled joint (fig.6) is basically a butt joint reinforced with dowels. Both halves of a joint are drilled at once to make the holes line up.

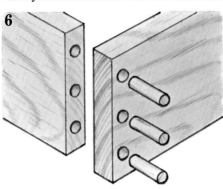
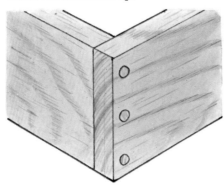

The mitred joint (fig.7) has a very neat appearance because no end grain is visible. It needs to be nailed or glued. Unfortunately, it is a very weak joint unless it is reinforced in some way.

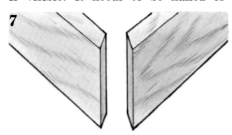

A halving joint (fig.8) is used at the corners of a rectangular frame. It is simple to make, has a reasonably neat appearance and is quite strong if glued together.

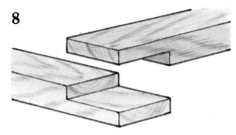
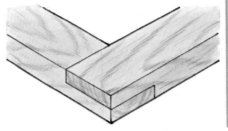

A breadboard

If you find a beautifully grained piece of hardwood, remember that the simplest designs are usually the most effective. This way the grain, colour and texture of the wood can be fully enjoyed.

To get familiar with working with hardwood and using the tools, make this handsome board—it can double as a cheese board.

The board is about 25.5cm x 35.5cm (10"x14")—it depends on how much wood is removed by planing. You can of course use the same idea to make a smaller or larger board. Try to obtain hardwood with interesting grain.

You will need:
Plane, marking gauge.
A piece of hardwood, or off-cuts, 19mm (¾") thick, from which to cut a piece 25.5cm (10") wide and 30.5cm (12") long, and two pieces 2.5cm (1") wide and 25.5cm (10") long—PBS. 4 pieces of 6mm (¼") dowelling, 5cm (2") long.
Hand drill with 6mm (¼") bit.
Tourniquet—old tights are ideal as they won't damage the wood.
Saw.
Fine grade glasspaper.
Wood glue.
Wax or linseed oil.

1. Measure and cut the hardwood to the sizes shown.

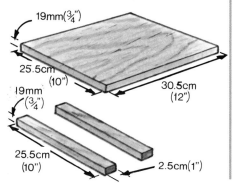

2. Assemble the pieces as shown and make sure that they fit snugly all round. Plane and smooth each piece of wood as necessary.

3. Glue and clamp the pieces together with a tourniquet made from tights.

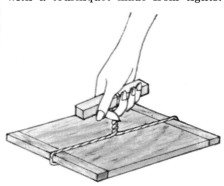

4. Drill holes 4cm (1½″) from the ends. The holes must be straight and go through into the larger piece for about 13mm (½″).

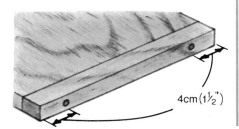

5. Insert pieces of dowel into the holes. They must go the length of the hole. Use a bit of wood glue if necessary. Trim and smooth the ends with fine grade glasspaper.

6. Wax or oil the board to finish.

The strips at the end of the board are joined with bits of dowelling rod.

Minimum-cost picture frames made to measure

Once you have become familiar with the basic techniques, the scope of carpentry widens very rapidly and you may well find that seemingly difficult things are now within your grasp.

The most important result of learning carpentry is that it enables you to make so many of the things that are very expensive to buy.

Picture frames are particularly expensive to have specially made because there is a lot of hand work involved, but they are relatively easy and quick to make. Once you have made frames for all your own prints and pictures, you'll doubtless find friends who have something they want to frame.

There are a variety of shapes available in ready-made mouldings that can be purchased from hardware stores, do-it-yourself shops etc.

There are several ways of connecting the pieces at the corner of a frame but for picture frames the mitre joint is usually used (fig.A).

The most difficult part to do is to get the opposite pieces of the frame exactly the same length. The only way to do this is to take care and learn from your mistakes.

Practise sawing and measuring on short bits of moulding or ordinary wood to get the feel of it.

The mitre is simply the term for two pieces of wood joined at right angles after they have been sawn at 45°.

There are several ways of joining the pieces but the easiest is the nail and

Small picture framed with a mounting board. Supplied by Blackman Harvey.

Tool box

Mitre box. If you intend to make several frames a mitre box is essential. It is inexpensive and can be bought from hardware stores.

Mark the mitre box by placing the saw

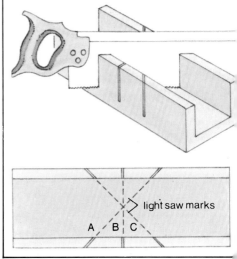

light saw marks

A B C

A

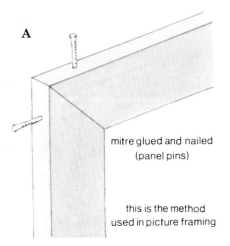

mitre glued and nailed
(panel pins)

this is the method
used in picture framing

A mitre joint, glued and nailed, is the method used for making frames.

glue technique used by most picture framers. The step demanding the most care is the nailing itself for it is a little difficult to keep the two 45° surfaces from sliding. It helps if you first glue the pieces and let them dry in position with a string loop all round the edge, to hold the frame secure before nailing the corners.

Decide how you want the frame to look. You may have maps or prints from old books that, because of their size, need small, delicate frames with the wood painted white, black or an antique gold. Initially buy ready-made moulding which comes in a variety of shapes and finishes to suit your purposes.

Various shapes and sizes of mouldings. Supplied by Blackman Harvey.

in each of the three slots in turn and make a slight mark in each direction on the base of the box. These will be used as guide lines in measuring. If you are using a bench hook, instead of a mitre box, carefully mark two 45° lines and cut a groove along each one as shown. Use a protractor to measure the 45° angle or use a compass and bisect a 90° angle. Saw and mark each piece as for the mitre box.

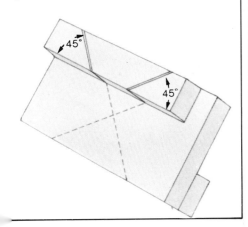

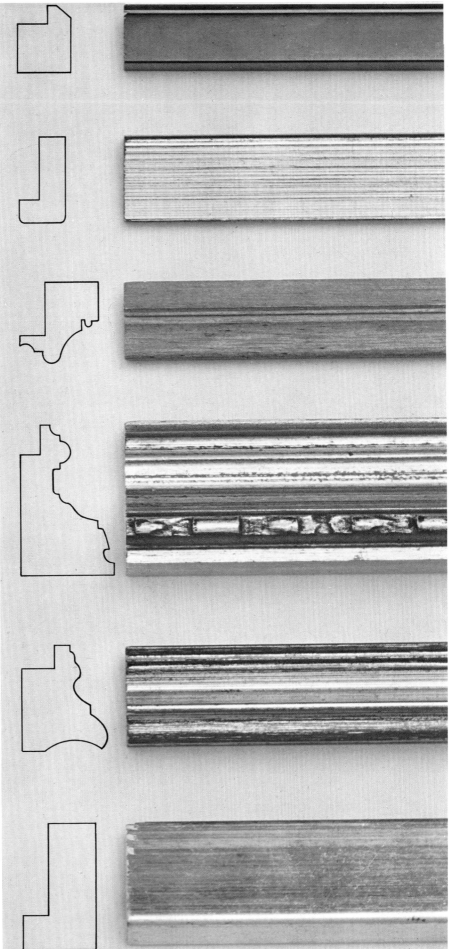

To make a picture frame

You will need:

Tools
Steel ruler

Mitre box

Panel saw—it must be a fine saw with 0.3m-0.4m (12-14points); a rough saw will have a lesser number of points. A fine tenon saw will do

Nylon cord—about 2m (2yd) for holding frame together while glue dries.

Nail punch

Hammer

Materials
Picture frame moulding: add 10cm (4″) to each dimension of the picture and add up the 4 lengths. Thus for a 30cm x 40cm (12″x16″) frame you will need 1.8m (72″) of 10mm (⅜″) half-round moulding (fig.B). The moulding can be bought from hardware stores, timber merchants and do-it-yourself shops

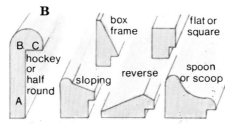

Picture frame moulding can be bought in various sizes and shapes.

Mounting board: if the picture is not going to fill the entire frame use a mounting board to surround the area between the picture and the frame

Glass: 2mm thick (18oz). Have this cut to size by a glass merchant or hardware store. Determine the size after the frame is assembled

Backing board: same size as the glass—any stiff cardboard will do

Panel pins: fine 19mm (¾″): about 24

2 hooks or staples to hold the wire

Wire: picture hanging wire, usually brass, can be bought from large department stores

Fine grade glasspaper

Wood glue

---

1. Measure the size of the picture to get the frame size. The size of the frame is the dimensions of the inside of the rebate—ie, the size of the glass and the backing cardboard. Assume the size to be 30cm x 40cm (12″x16″).

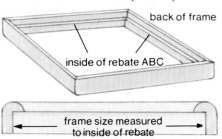

2. Cut off one end of moulding as shown, with back against side of mitre box. Start sawing towards yourself with the saw tilting forwards a little. Then level the saw and with easy, unhurried strokes saw off the end as shown.

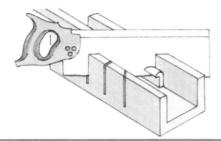

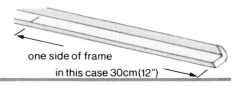

hold moulding firmly against side of mitre block

3. Measure and mark the piece of moulding as shown.

one side of frame
in this case 30cm(12″)

---

4. Match this mark with line C as shown and saw through the moulding. Repeat this to get an identical piece. It is essential that the lengths are exactly the same.

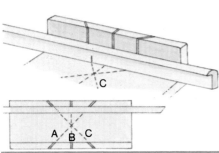

5. Carefully measure and saw two pieces 40cm (16″) long.

6. Sand the cut ends of the pieces lightly to remove rough edges. Use fine glasspaper with a sanding block.

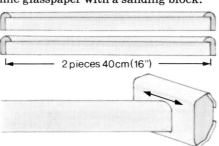

2 pieces 40cm(16″)

7. Prepare the nylon cord by tying a slip knot. This can then be tightened around the frame by pulling one end.

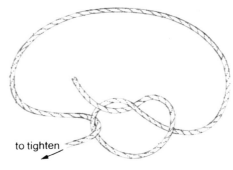

to tighten

---

8. Glue the frame together. Put a dab of glue on each end and smooth it with a piece of wood. Arrange the four pieces together with cord round them.

9. Tighten cord, adjusting corners as you tighten. Leave to dry.

10. When dry, remove the cord and nail in panel pins as shown. Nail carefully, holding the side receiving the nail very firmly against a flat working surface. Use a nail punch to set nails slightly below surface of wood.

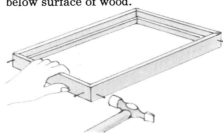

11. Take measurements of the back of the frame and order glass to fit. Cut the backing board (and mounting board if necessary) to fit inside. Wax, stain or paint the frame.

Assembling picture frame

12. Mounting board is only necessary if the picture is smaller than the frame. Clean the glass, then assemble as shown. Glue the picture with rubber-based cement to the backing board or, if it is too valuable or thin, place it between the layers and hold it in position while carefully assembling the picture. If the backing is stiff and cut to the right size it will hold the picture in position once the backing board is secured.

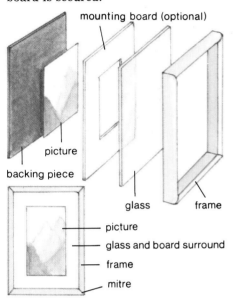

13. Nail panel pins on the inside back of the frame to hold the layers down firmly. Leave 6mm ($\frac{1}{4}$") sticking out. To prevent dust collecting, cover the entire back with brown paper.

14. Put in hooks or staples. Attach the wire securely to the hooks so that the wire will not slip loose. Do not leave the wire ends too long or they will stick out from the frame.

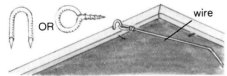

The completed frames can be finished in different ways. They can be left natural or you can paint them with gloss or matt paint. Designed by A. Martensson.

Planning and fitting out your work area

A well designed working area makes it easy to keep things tidy and for clearing up afterwards. When planning a work room two of the most important factors are the source of light and power.
If you are right-handed keep the light to your left or in front and above you. Tool storage must be so arranged that you can reach things easily without the possibility of knocking things over in the course of your work.

The problem with creating a working surface is not only the expense but finding the necessary space. A working surface or a work bench does not have to be large nor expensive to be effective. The essential thing is that the working area must be suited to the purpose for which it is intended. A work bench must be steady and also large enough to allow you to work on it with ease. For example, if you are sawing you will need some elbow space and room to move the saw in its cutting position. This does not necessarily mean that the surface must be large. If it is kept uncluttered by tools and materials, quite a lot can be done on a very small area.

Tool storage. Keep tools near at hand. If each tool has its place on a shelf and is within easy reach, it is easier to clean and tidy the working area. Various space-saving suggestions for storing tools are made towards the end of this chapter.

Make-do surfaces. Most flats, apartments or houses contain something with a good surface that is steady enough for doing odd jobs, but the problem is that this surface is not always suitable for holding clamps ór vices and is liable to be damaged by them. However, it is easy to protect a surface from being damaged by clamps and vices if you use a piece of hardwood —any odd bit—between the clamp and the surface. Another alternative is to use a vice with built-in suction pads rather than a metal clamping device. The working surface should be free of nails or screws on the upper surface so that when you are using cutting tools there is no chance of damaging their cutting edges or blades on screws or nails. While natural wood is usually used in preference to man-made boards for working surfaces a similar thickness of blockboard can be used or, if available, multi-ply is also suitable. The advantage of using man-made boards is that they will not warp.

Work benches to buy

Work benches can be bought in different sizes and shapes, depending very much on how much you want to spend. The cheapest commercially-available bench is a saw horse (fig.1). If you have two of these they can be used to support a top to make a table or a work top on which to stand when painting and decorating. If you can find an old door, cover it with plywood to give you a flat surface. It makes a good work top when placed on the saw horses.

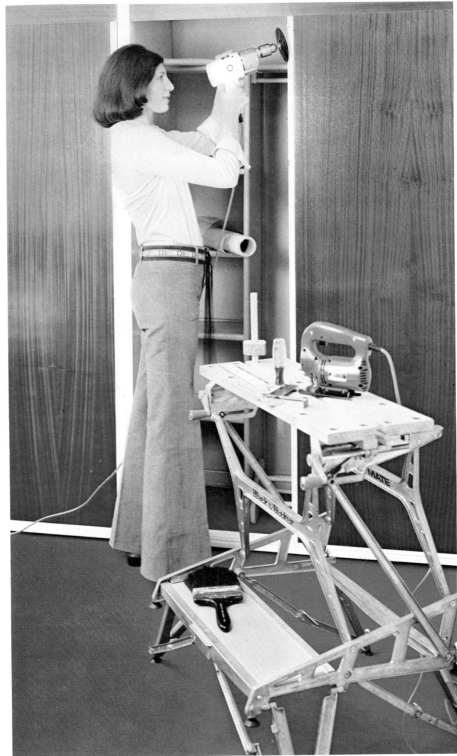

The Workmate is a versatile, commercially-available work bench. It has two working levels and a built-in vice and it can be folded almost flat.

Wood or metal benches in various sizes are also available commercially. Whatever your choice for a work bench make sure that it is suitable for your work. It is pointless buying the most expensive one if you are not going to make full use of it, besides you may find more satisfaction in making your own work surface for your craft.

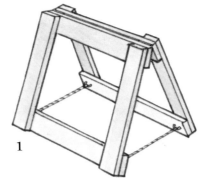

1

1. Two saw horses combined with a strong flat surface makes a good work bench. It can double as a kitchen table or it can be used to stand on when painting and decorating.

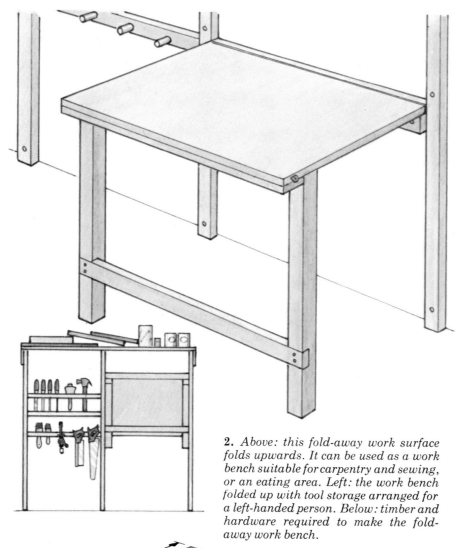

Fold-away surfaces

A working surface which folds away is very useful and space-saving but it must be constructed properly otherwise it will not be steady. This type of workbench can be installed anywhere where it is possible to attach battens to the wall and where marks made on the wall behind during work will not matter unduly.

The fold-away work surface (fig.2) can be part of a wall storage unit. To make a fold-away work surface first decide on how high you want it to be—the height must be relative to your own height so that you can work comfortably without having to stoop—76cm (30″) is about average. The area of the working surface must be large enough for your particular work without taking up too much space within the surrounding area.

The measurements for the fold-away work surface in the following instructions will make a working area 91.5cm x 61cm (3′x2′), 76cm (30″) high. You can vary the size to suit yourself.

You will need:

Timber

Blockboard 91.5cm x 61cm (3′x2′), 25mm (1″) thick.

The lengths given for the softwood are exact. Buy the timber slightly longer and trim it to size as you work. This allows for squaring the ends and trimming the legs, if necessary, to level the working surface.

Softwood 50mm x 50mm (2″x2″), 91.5cm (36″) long—for the batten against the wall.

2 pieces of softwood 50mm x 50mm (2″x2″), 73.5cm (29″) long—for the legs.

Softwood 25mm x 25mm (1″x1″), 91.5cm (36″) long—strip above batten to hold work surface.

Softwood 25mm x 75mm (1″x3″), 91.5cm (36″) long—to reinforce the front edge of the work surface.

Softwood 25mm x 50mm (1″x2″), 91.5cm (36″) long—for the strip between the legs.

Hardware

2 hinges with screws—to attach the legs to the blockboard—a 4.5cm (1¾″) back flap hinge with uncranked knuckle or table leaf hinges, are suitable.

Continuous hinge or Hurlinge, with screws to attach the blockboard to batten.

Set hinges as described in the chapter on making boxes.

4 screws 9cm (3½″) long—to attach the batten to the wall.

4 screws 4cm (1½″) long—to attach cross-piece to legs.

2 gate hooks or cabin hooks—these are attached to wall plugs and hook into the work surface when folded away to secure it.

Wood glue.

2. Above: this fold-away work surface folds upwards. It can be used as a work bench suitable for carpentry and sewing, or an eating area. Left: the work bench folded up with tool storage arranged for a left-handed person. Below: timber and hardware required to make the fold-away work bench.

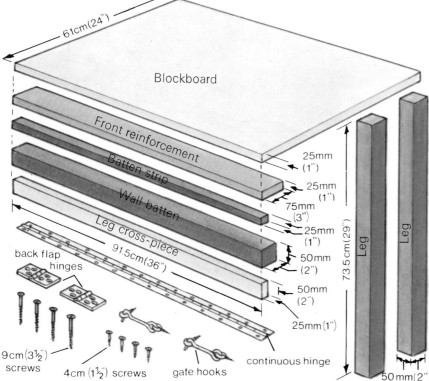

☐ Glue the reinforcement strip of wood to the front underside of the blockboard. Clamp and leave to dry.

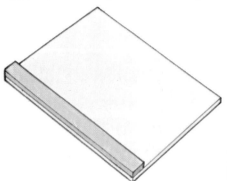

☐ Using a file round the opposite edge on the underside of the blockboard. This gives the necessary clearance to fold the surface away.

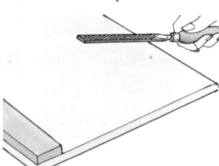

☐ Attach the strip hinge or Hurlinge to the blockboard.

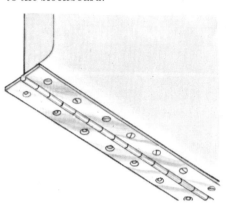

☐ Attach the leg cross-piece to the legs so that it is 15cm (6″) from the leg ends. Set the cross-piece into the front of the legs by making saw cuts to the required depth and then remove the waste with a chisel.

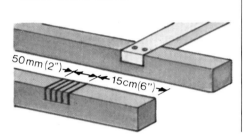

☐ Round top front edge of legs to allow for hinge clearance when folding up.

☐ Attach the legs to the underside of the blockboard with hinges.

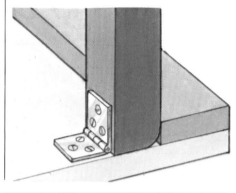

☐ Glue the batten strip to the wall batten as shown.

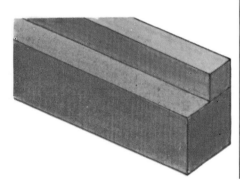

☐ Attach the batten to the wall with 9cm (3½″) screws. Make sure that its position is such that when the working surface rests on it, the working surface will be level (use a spirit level if necessary).

☐ Screw the hinge on the blockboard to the batten against the wall to assemble the work bench.

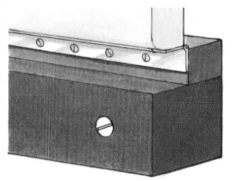

☐ Attach one eyelet to each side edge of the work surface. Fold the surface upwards and make marks on the wall corresponding to the eyelets. Insert wall plugs at the marks and attach gate hooks or cabin hooks to complete.

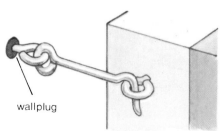

wallplug

You can adapt the design to build a breakfast bar.

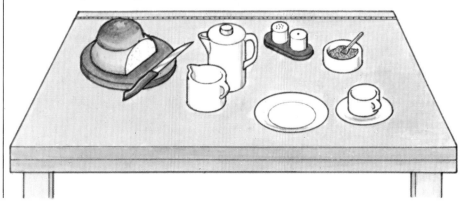

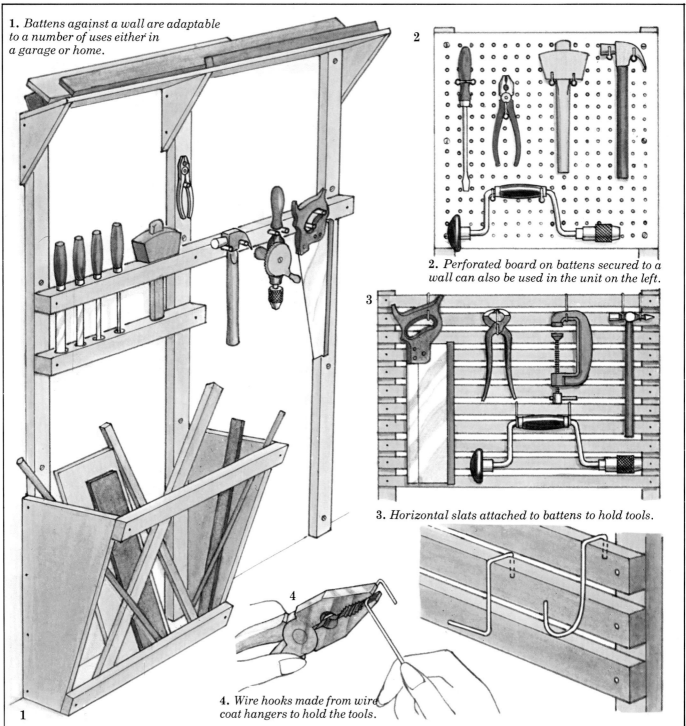

1. Battens against a wall are adaptable to a number of uses either in a garage or home.

2. Perforated board on battens secured to a wall can also be used in the unit on the left.

3. Horizontal slats attached to battens to hold tools.

4. Wire hooks made from wire coat hangers to hold the tools.

Wall storage

Vertical battens screwed to the wall can be used as the basis of a tool-storage system, tailor-made to your own requirements and capable of expansion. One possible design is shown in fig.1. Planes, boxes and tins can be stored on shelves, while any odd pieces of wood can be kept in an improvised bin which is easily made from plywood. Chisels are inserted through one piece of wood with their sharp ends covered, and rest in holes drilled in another. If you hang up a saw, make sure that the teeth are protected by a wooden or plastic scabbard.

Perforated hardboard panels

Another useful idea is to screw a perforated hardboard sheet to the battens and then buy special hooks to hold your tools (fig.2).

Horizontal slats

Alternatively you can devise your own hanging space by nailing or screwing 12mm x 25mm ($\frac{1}{2}$"x1") horizontal strips to the battens, leaving a space of about 12mm ($\frac{1}{2}$") between them (fig.3). You can then fashion hanging hooks in any shape by bending lengths of wire coat-hanger with a pair of pliers (fig.

4). File the ends of the wire smooth or double up the hook so that both ends will be at the back.

Another possibility is to drill holes at a downward angle into the slats and insert pieces of dowel rod so that they slant upwards.

The advantage of using the horizontal slat method is that it is attractive enough to put up in a kitchen or hallway, and it can be used to hang up anything. In the kitchen it makes a wonderful place to arrange your utensils, in the study you can hang pencil containers and small boxes for other odds and ends.

Above: this versatile hang-up unit is suitable for the kitchen or workshop. It consists of a frame held together with halving joints. Right: a smaller unit is useful for sewing materials.

A hang-up unit

This versatile storage unit can be used in a kitchen, study or garage. The overall size is 91.4cm x 68.6cm (36″x27″). It consists of a framework, cross slats and back supports. The frame is joined together by halving joints.

You will need:
Panel saw.
Carpenter's square.
Screwdriver and hammer. Hand drill.
4 screws 31mm (1¼″) long.
32 screws 25mm (1″) long.
Wood glue and glasspaper.
Polyurethane varnish, panel pins.
Softwood 51mm x 19mm (2″x¾″), 3.3m (11′) long.
Softwood 76mm x 19mm (3″x¾″), 1.42m (56″) long.
Softwood 51mm x 51mm (2″x2″), 22cm (8¾″) long.
Softwood 25mm x 19mm (1″x¾″), 15m (16yd) long—from which to cut 16 horizontal slats each 87cm (34¼″) long.

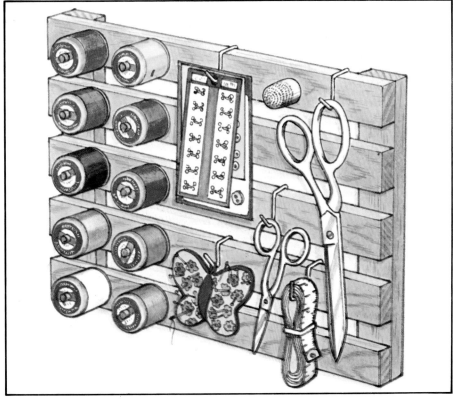

1. To make the frame cut the lengths of softwood indicated.
A halving joint is used to join two pieces of wood together.

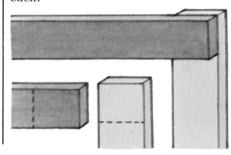

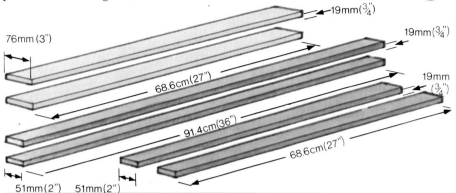

2. To make the halving joint place two pieces at right angles to each other and mark the width of each piece of wood on to the other. The mark on the vertical piece will be on the front and on the horizontal piece it will be at the back.

3. Using the saw cut along this line through exactly half the thickness of the wood.

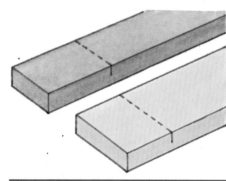

4. Along the width of the cross section draw a line to halve the thickness and cut down this line to the previous saw cut.

5. Repeat this with the other ends of the frame. Assemble the frame as shown.

back view

6. From the front drill a hole at each corner. Glue the frame together. Insert 31mm (1¼″) screws through the joins and into the square pieces to secure it.

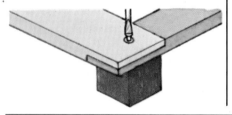

7. Nail the side pieces (also known as fillets) to the square pieces.

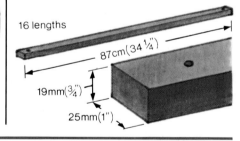

8. Cut 16 lengths as shown.
9. Drill a hole through each end of these pieces.

16 lengths

87cm(34¼″)

19mm(¾″)

25mm(1″)

10. Glue and screw the 16 pieces to the back of the frame. Make sure that the slats are parallel and evenly spaced.
11. Drill a hole 25mm (1″) deep in each of the square pieces along the top of the frame. Measure the distance between the two holes and drill corresponding holes in the surface on which the frame will hang. Plug the holes and insert 50mm (2″) screws so that half the length of the screw protrudes from the wall and hang the unit.

A simple box construction to hang on the unit. Glue, nail or screw it together and add metal brackets to the back to hook box on to the slats.

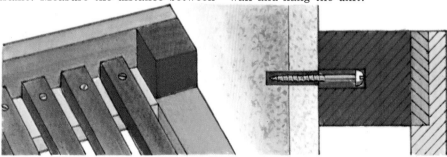

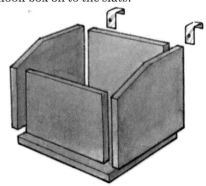

The care and maintenance of tools

The simplest way of dealing with the problem of tool maintenance is to make sure that you keep the need for it to the minimum. This can be achieved in various ways. Store tools properly, use them for their intended purpose and do not drop them nor knock them about. Even with the most careful and knowledgeable treatment, most kinds of tools need a little attention from time to time to keep them at their best. Apart from abuse, there are two other chief enemies.

Rust. Good storage conditions are essential to keep rust at bay. Even in a 'dry' place, condensation can occur when it is cold unless the tools are in close proximity to rust-inhibiting paper or coated with oil or lacquer. Linseed oil is suitable for coating tools (not as a lubricant). Apply it with a wad of cottonwool.

If rust has appeared on a tool, steel wool and fine oil will take it off without much trouble. Rust that is too heavy or thick for this treatment may well have ruined the tool.

Wear. Most good tools should last a

There is little chance of good work being done in this workshop!

lifetime, and many improve with age. What wears out many tools is not hard work but sheer lack of lubrication. Tools do not need much oil—quite the contrary—but they do need the right kind and in the right places.

Lubricants

Little and often is a good rule. If a tool is used every day or once a week, its working parts could do with a drop or two; once a month is a good idea anyway, whether the tool is used or not, because the fine oil used contains a high proportion of paraffin and tends to dry out to some extent.

To obtain a suitable oil for your tools read the label of contents on the can and avoid those containing molybdenum or graphite and if in doubt ask your hardware dealer for advice. A good all-purpose oil, such as 3-in-One, is useful and also suitable for a sewing machine.

Hand drills and braces themselves need only light oiling in the moving parts including the brace head mountings and chuck threads. There is no need to dismantle the tool, a drop of oil will work its way through.

Power tools should have their lead cable and motor professionally examined after every fifty hours of use. This may mean having the tool serviced every six months or (as is more likely) every two years, according to the amount of use it gets. A power tool should not be allowed to work indefinitely just because it is going well. Do not oil or grease a power tool; if you do and it's not in the right places it can do more harm than good. If a power tool is serviced at regular intervals there is no need for further lubricating.

Benches and clamps

Your work bench is a tool, a gripping device and a reference for edge and surface flatness. If a bench is used with care, the occasional going over with a finely set plane should be all it needs apart from oiling or lacquering.

A very rough or uneven top may be better covered with a new, thick section board: chipboard is especially suitable, being very flat and relatively inexpensive.

If a vice jams or rocks about it can be more of a hindrance than a help to you. So tighten structural bolts or screws from time to time. Partially dismount the vice to clean and oil it.

Replace wooden jaw linings before they are so damaged as to mark your timber. Use a hardwood such as beech to replace the wooden linings. Cut the lining to the size of the one being removed and screw or bolt it back.

G-clamps. A little oil on the thread and in the small ball-joint at the screw-end foot should be all that a G-clamp needs. G-clamps are made from malleable iron, so if you have dropped one and knocked it out of line it is possible to hammer it carefully back straight.

Striking tools

Apart from screwdrivers, hammers and mallets are subject to the worst abuse. **Hammers** need frequent checking to ensure the fit of handle to head, not because they are shoddily made (assuming you have bought a reputable brand—which is always advisable) but because of the way they are used.

Once a head is loose, do not be tempted into dunking the tool in a bucket of water. This only swells the fibres in the confined space of the hammer eye and destroys their strength. Have the handle replaced or, if the head is worn as well, replace the hammer with a new one before it does someone harm. Keep an eye on the striking face. Any signs of cracks or chipping anywhere on the head indicate that it is time to get a replacement. A chip flying from a faulty hammer face can reach the velocity of a bullet and do a great deal of damage. Keep the striking surfaces clean by rubbing them with abrasive paper.

Mallets are made from hardwood, usually beech, so they appreciate an occasional drop of linseed oil to stop them drying out. Looseness of heads is cured simply by tapping the tool upside down on a firm surface, as the head is self-wedging on to the handle.

Screwdriving tools

The two main types are hand screwdrivers and spiral-ratchet screwdrivers. Each type includes screwdrivers of various sizes to cope with the appropriate screws.

As far as possible, try to match the screwdriver tip to the screw slot to prevent damage to either of them.

Hand screwdrivers should have their tips filed true when there is any sign of rounding or damage. Small screwdrivers used on large screws are easily damaged. A screwdriver is meant to fit snugly into screw slots. Ideally, they should be fat enough not to go quite down to the bottom of the screw slot.

To reface a screwdriver clamp it in a vice (use bits of waste wood to protect wooden jaw linings if necessary). Use a flat metal-work file and file the front end flat and square. Then trim each of the four sides in turn.

Spiral ratchets need only the occasional drop or two of oil in the chuck sleeve. Pull the chuck sleeve as if inserting a bit, and drop the oil in the small space at the front. The oil will work its way gradually back to the ratchet mechanism.

Tool box

Hammers

The right tool for the job makes all the difference. To most people a hammer is simply a tool to drive a nail home. However, different hammers vary in their function and each type is available in various weights. Some of the more common hammers illustrated have a specific function.

Claw hammer, 200gm-850gm (7oz-30oz), is used for general purpose carpentry, particularly for driving and removing nails. When removing nails make sure that the nail is well into the claw, then lever evenly.

Warrington or cross pein hammer, 170gm-450gm (6oz-16oz), is used for general nailing, joinery, and planishing or metal beating.

Ball pein or engineer's hammer, 110gm-1360gm (4oz-3lb), is used for metal working. The round end is for starting rivets; its face is hardened steel and will not chip.

Pin or telephone hammer, 100gm-110gm (3½oz-4oz), is used for tacks, panel pins and fine nailing. The wedge shaped end is used for starting small nails while holding them between the fingers.

Mallets

There are two basic types of mallet. **Carpentry mallet,** used in carpentry and cabinet making. **Carver's mallet,** used for creative woodwork.

Screwdrivers

Standard slotted screwdriver is used for general driving of single slotted screws.

Spiral ratchet screwdriver is used for general purpose screwdriving. By pushing in the handle it automatically drives or removes screws. When locked the ratchet allows screw to be driven or removed without taking the tip from the screw slot. Bits of different sizes can be fitted into the chuck, making this a very versatile tool.

Crosshead screwdriver, also known as Phillips, is used with cross slotted screws to provide greater grip between the tip and the screw head.

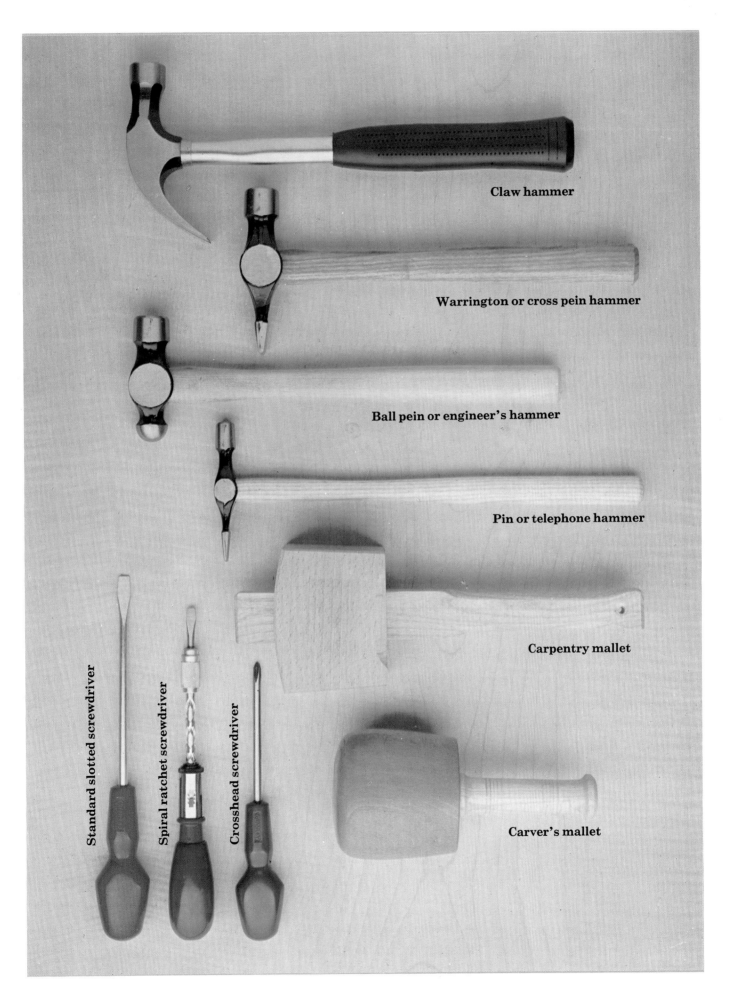

Claw hammer

Warrington or cross pein hammer

Ball pein or engineer's hammer

Pin or telephone hammer

Carpentry mallet

Standard slotted screwdriver

Spiral ratchet screwdriver

Crosshead screwdriver

Carver's mallet

How to keep the cutting edges sharp

No matter how well you look after tools, some will require further attention. Cutting tools, such as saws, chisels, drill bits, files and planes will need sharpening from time to time. It is possible to sharpen some of them but others, such as saws, are best left to those qualified to do so.

Sharpening materials

There are various tools and materials available for cleaning and sharpening tools. But the two most often used for sharpening at home are the grinding wheel and oilstone.

Grinding wheel. A small, powered grinding wheel is any handyman's or woman's companion. If you have one use a wheel-dressing tool to trim the edges and keep the wheels cutting freely. A clogged wheel invites excess pressure, making the tool extremely dangerous. Replace the wheels before they become impractically small in diameter, and check the tightness of the mounting nuts when a new wheel has been running for a short while. There is no need to heave on the nuts at all heavily, since they are self-tightening, once nipped firmly home.

Oilstones. A whetstone is a fine grained stone used for sharpening tools. Oil is used on the stone, hence oilstone, to protect and clean the surface. Do not flood the stone with oil, but do cover it with a thin film. The job of the oil is not to lubricate the action but to suspend the metal particles that the stone removes, floating them above its surface so that they can be wiped off with absorbent rag or paper. Don't use the same rag over and over, or you will rub the swarf (chips and filings) into the stone. Small flecks of metal embedded in the stone will ruin it—and there is nothing you can do to save it.
Keep the surface clean. It is no use trying to scrub out the swarf every now and then; it must be done after each sharpening job.

Saws

Saws should be sharpened by professionals. If you use the correct saw for the cut being made the saw will give you good service and will not require frequent sharpening.

When doing small odd jobs, especially with softwoods, the type of saw used is not very important as satisfactory results can be obtained with almost any saw. However, when doing larger jobs, especially if a hardwood is being used, it becomes more important to use a specific type of saw. The right saw for the right job not only gives better results but also makes the cutting easier.
Each type of saw is available with different blades and although the blades are the same size and similar in appearance, it is the number and the angle of the teeth (points) which give it a specific purpose.

Points refer to the number of saw teeth per 2.5cm (1″) of a blade. Woodworking saws with a small number of points are suitable for softwoods and a larger number of points are required for hardwoods.

The gullet is the distance between one point and the next. The gullet carries the sawdust out of the saw cut. Softwoods produce more waste so the saw should have a larger gullet than a saw used for cutting hardwoods.

Hand saw—(fig.1) there are three types of hand saws:
A rip saw, 3-6 points, is used for cutting softwoods with the grain.
Cross-cut saw, 5-10 points, is used for cutting across the grain of softwoods and hardwoods.
Panel saw, 7-12 points, is used for fine sawing and some joints. It is suitable for cutting softwoods and hardwoods. It can also be used on plywood, blockboard and hardboard. Do remember that the glue content in man-made boards is hard wearing on cutting tools so, as far as possible, have them cut to size when purchasing.
Tenon or back saw—(fig.2) is used for general carpentry, cutting across the grain on small pieces of wood and for joints.
Other saws such as flooring saws are special purpose tools and the home craftsman or woman will have no need for them. Other special purpose saws include coping saws, fret saws and bow saws—these all have replaceable blades so sharpening is no problem and the chances are that the blade will break before it needs sharpening.

Saw sharpening is really for the professional. It can be done with a fair degree of success by the really experienced home craftsman or woman, but it is a time-consuming job, requiring special triangular files, clamping devices and an expensive saw setting tool. Since saws need attention so very infrequently in normal use, maintaining them yourself is scarcely worth the trouble.

Files

These need early mention, since they are used extensively in maintaining other tools. They are themselves easily maintained.
Surform tools, which work rather like kitchen shredders, need no maintenance apart from the occasional clearance of accumulated shavings which clog up their action, particularly in the case of the round Surforms which have a very small trap for the swarf.
Files need to be carded (cleaned with a fine wire brush) from time to time.
Carding gives files a new lease of life, especially when they have been used on soft metals such as copper and aluminium. File cards are readily available in tool shops.
File handles need to be examined for signs of cracking. A handle that is split makes a file a potentially dangerous tool because when it gives way in use the sharp tang (the part inside the handle) can be driven into the hand or wrist. Safety-type handles are widely sold, and are not expensive. They may be made of plastic or hardwood with special reinforcement embedded inside the handle.

Chisels

There are two main types of chisel.
A bevel edged chisel (fig.3) is used to remove wood in awkward corners. The sloping sides make it easier to work in a confined space.
A firmer chisel (fig.4) is more generally used. It can be hit with a mallet whereas a bevel edged chisel should never be hit with a mallet. However, specially made chisels in the shape of a bevel edged chisel can be hit with a mallet—they are referred to as a firmer bevel edged chisel.
Plastic handles are very strong and practically indestructible and therefore safe. If chisels have wooden handles check them occasionally for splits and make sure they are securely attached (if you have tools from a reputable tool manufacturer you should not have any problems).
Sharpening. Firmer chisels and bevel edged chisels are similarly sharpened. The angle of the bevel to the oilstone must be constant—about 30° (fig.5). If it is not constant the cutting edge will form a curve.

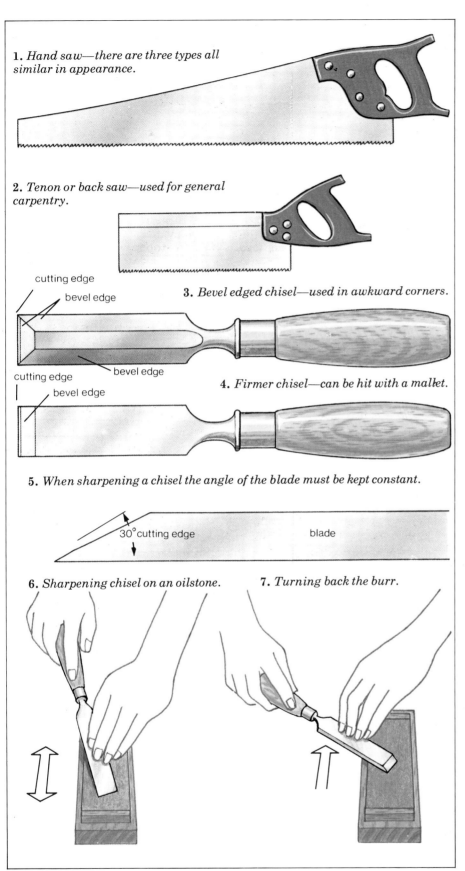

1. *Hand saw—there are three types all similar in appearance.*

2. *Tenon or back saw—used for general carpentry.*

cutting edge
bevel edge

3. *Bevel edged chisel—used in awkward corners.*

cutting edge
bevel edge

4. *Firmer chisel—can be hit with a mallet.*

cutting edge
bevel edge

5. *When sharpening a chisel the angle of the blade must be kept constant.*

30° cutting edge   blade

6. *Sharpening chisel on an oilstone.*   7. *Turning back the burr.*

A honing guide can be used to keep the angle constant. It is normally used when sharpening plane blades. Try to obtain one that is suitable for chisels as well.
The chisel is moved backwards and forwards, bevel side down, on the oilstone. You can save a great deal of uneven wear on the oilstone by saving its face for wide chisels and doing narrower ones along the sides of the oilstone.

Sharpening without a honing guide.
Lower the chisel handle until you can feel the bevel flat on the stone. Raise the handle end by about 25mm (1") and you will have the honing angle about right. Keep your wrists rigid and move only from elbows and shoulder joints while moving the chisel backwards and forwards (fig.6). A burr (rough edge) will form on the edge which you should be able to feel if you draw your thumb across the back edge. Remove the burr by laying the blade flat side down on the stone and wiping it obliquely off (fig.7). You should be able to see the burr lying on the stone. Feel carefully (ie stroking with your palm going away from the edge, not towards it nor along it) to find if some of the burr has been bent over to the back. If it has, stroke the bevel and the back lightly on the stone alternately with single strokes, so as to repeat the honing action, until the burr has disappeared.
Be very careful during this operation not to rub bits of burr into the stone; use a clear part of it, or wipe and re-oil the stone.
The chisel should now be perfectly sharp. You should not be able to see any vestige, looking at the edge head-on, of the fine silver thread that betrays a blunt edge.

Planes
Plane blades are sharpened exactly the same as chisel edges. Use a honing guide if possible and try to retain the same angle on the cutting edge as the original. Check the type of plane you are using and set the honing guide to the angle recommended for your plane by the manufacturers.
If you are using a plane with replaceable blades, the problem of sharpening does not arise as you simply insert a new blade.

Knives
Most knives have throw-away blades, but they can be sharpened on an oilstone edge. The twin bevels on the knife are normally set at about 25° to the blade sides, and need to be sharpened evenly so that one side does not become wider than the other. Do not sharpen knife blades square to the stone edge, but obliquely. You will not risk digging into the stone surface. The burr from a knife edge is very fine, but it is still there, so the same care is needed as when sharpening the very obviously burred planes and chisels.

Drill bits
Sharpening twist drill bits and masonry bits is another job best left to experts. Unless the angles are precisely right, any attempt at sharpening is more likely to cause harm.

Tile~top coffee table with simple joints

A coffee table is easily made with simple joints. The design for the table illustrated is based on two much used joints —the halving joint and the mitred joint.

For those inexperienced in making any type of joint at all, a sawing jig such as a Jointmaster, brings these simple joints within everybody's capabilities. The sawing jig can also be used to make more complicated joins.

If the instructions are followed carefully a professional finish is practically guaranteed. There is however, no substitute for accurate measuring and marking out, and special care should be taken at this stage if a pleasing construction is to be obtained.

The Table
The completed table is about 68.5cm (27″) square and is 35.5cm (14″) high.

The underframe is designed to hold a top with sixteen standard tiles—15cm (6″) square. However the size can be varied and the top can be made larger to overhang the underframe.
Construction of the underframe and the top are dealt with in separate stages. For the latter a wide choice of treatments is possible. For example, tapestry or collage can be used instead of tiles. All the materials are readily available

Frame for top

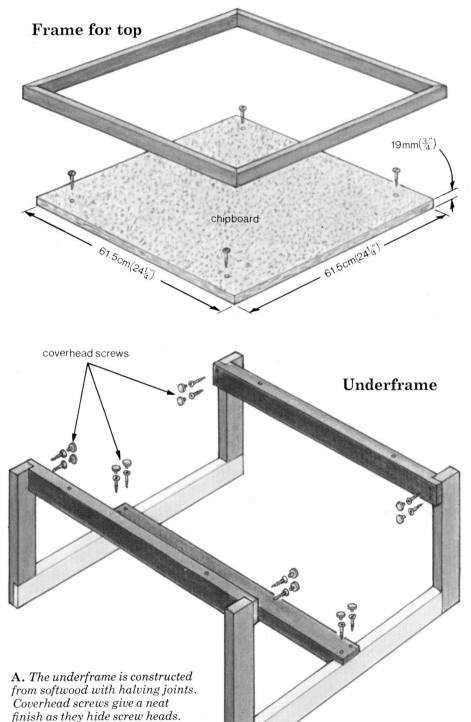

19mm($\frac{3}{4}$″)

chipboard

61.5cm(24$\frac{1}{4}$″)

61.5cm(24$\frac{1}{4}$″)

coverhead screws

Underframe

A. *The underframe is constructed from softwood with halving joints. Coverhead screws give a neat finish as they hide screw heads. The top is a mitred frame around chipboard.*

Left: softwood coffee table made with simple joints. Designer: Ron Kidd.

from timber merchants and DIY shops. The quality of timber can vary considerably so it is worth paying a little extra to select a timber with good grain. An extra length of timber (softwood) should be purchased and a few practice joints carried out so that you can get used to the sawing jig. Once you know how to make a good halving joint start on the underframe for the table.
Softwood—ask your timber merchant for 'joinery' softwood and have him plane it to the required cross-section (you might have to order it a day or two in advance).
Hardwood—these instructions are for softwood but you can use hardwood—which is more expensive—instead. You will need the same quantities and the method of construction is also the same.
Finishing—the finish is optional. If the table is made from a softwood it can be stained almost any colour with a wood stain, or the wood can be given a coat of matt or gloss polyurethane varnish.
A hardwood is best left matt, so seal the surface with a matt varnish or polish it with wax.
You will need:
Saw, carpenter's square, trimming knife, screwdriver, marking gauge, hammer and nail punch.
Drill with 3mm ($\frac{1}{8}$″) bit.
Sawing jig (optional).
Plane and fine grade glasspaper.
Vice or G-clamp.
Woodworking adhesive, wood stain or varnish to choice.
Tiles (optional) or other suitable inlay.
Tile adhesive, grout and plastic wood—for a tile top.
Hardware
12 No.8 coverhead screws 25mm (1″) long.
Four No.8 steel countersunk screws.
Panel pins—30mm (1$\frac{1}{4}$″) long and 16mm ($\frac{5}{8}$″) long.
Timber
50mm x 25mm (2″x 1″) softwood, overall length 600cm (20′). This is for the underframe (fig.A)—cut three pieces 72.5cm (28$\frac{1}{2}$″) long, two pieces 70cm (27$\frac{1}{2}$″) long and two pieces 67.5cm (26$\frac{1}{4}$″) long. These lengths are slightly long but it will make handling easier. The odd piece left after cutting the lengths indicated can be used for practising the halving joint.
25mm x 12mm (1″x $\frac{1}{2}$″) softwood, 275cm (9′) long—frame for top (fig.A)—cut into four equal lengths.
19mm ($\frac{3}{4}$″) chipboard, 61.5cm (24$\frac{1}{4}$″) square—for the top. This will hold 16 standard 15cm (6″) tiles but you can finish the top in any way you like.
If you use tiles, lay them out in a square and measure them so that you can buy the exact size of chipboard.

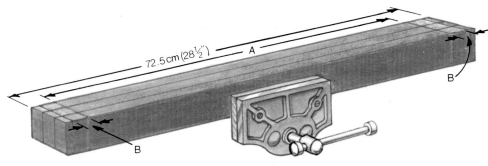

1. Clamp the three longest frame pieces of timber and mark out as shown. Use a trimming knife and mark all three pieces at the same time so that they are identical. Use the carpenter's square to ensure right angles.

A = length of chipboard plus twice thickness of timber for frame.

B = thickness of underframe timber

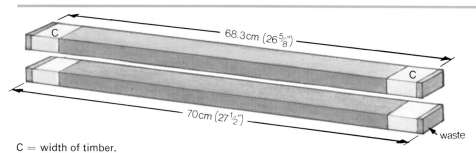

C = width of timber.

3. Similarly mark the two 70cm (27½") long pieces as shown but measuring the width and not the thickness.

5. Set the marking gauge to exactly half the thickness of the timber. Test this setting by marking on the timber from both sides. If the gauge is set to the exact half of the timber the marks will coincide. If a pair of lines show on the timber this means that the gauge is not set accurately and should be re-adjusted. Mark each end as shown.

centre line

6. Saw off the waste at the ends of each piece of timber, taking care to saw against the marked line on the waste side.

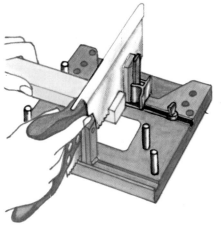

7. To make the halving joint cut the timber down the central line (on the waste side) on each end of each piece. Cut to make the ends as shown. The cut-outs must be made on the same surface of each piece of wood.

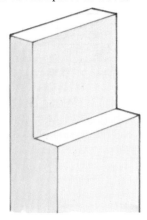

10. Once the frame is dry it is cut in half. Measure and cut carefully between the lines marked.

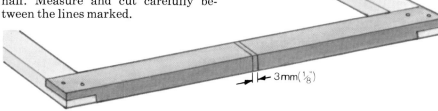

3mm(⅛")

11. Clean the three cross rails using glasspaper and bore two holes in each end for the coverhead screws.

12. Drill pilot holes and assemble the underframe (fig.A). Glue and screw the rails in position. Clean surfaces with glasspaper if necessary and stain or varnish.

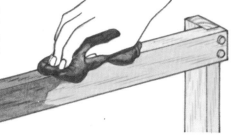

Coverhead screws hide screw heads from view. Covers are available in various shapes and finishes.

2. Square the lines from the edge across the wide surfaces and down the opposite edge.

waste

4. Repeat previous markings on the two remaining pieces as indicated.

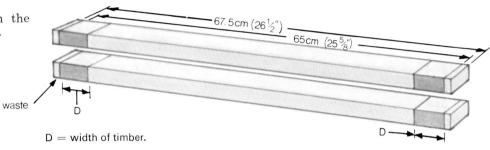

67.5cm (26½")

65cm (25⅝")

waste

D

D

D = width of timber.

8. The inside edges of the pieces must be cleaned and made smooth using either a plane or glasspaper.

9. The frame legs are assembled as a square and then cut in half. Glue and secure corners with the shorter panel

pins while the glue is still wet and set the heads below the surface using the nail punch. Wipe off excess glue.

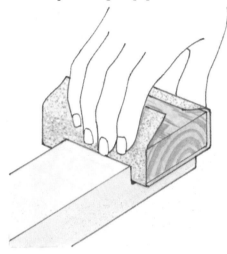

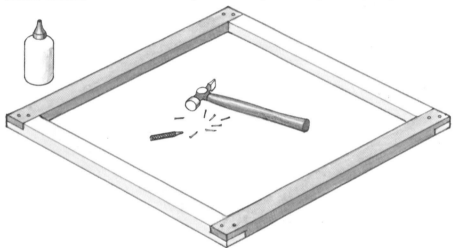

The frame to fit around the chipboard —for the top—is made with mitre joints. For details see next chapter which also explains frames suitable for tops using alternatives to tiles.

The completed underframe assembled with coverhead screws is ready to have a top fitted. The top is attached by screwing it to the two horizontal rails.

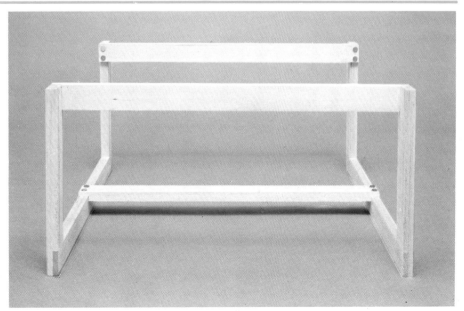

1. Measure the length of the chipboard, say 61.5cm (24¼″) and mark this length on to the four pieces of timber. Start measuring 2.5cm (1″) from the ends to allow for the mitres.

2. The lengths marked out will form the inside of the frame. Make the mitre cuts on the waste side of marks.

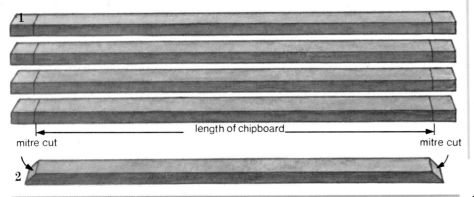

length of chipboard

mitre cut

mitre cut

The tile top

The dimensions of the underframe are such that it will hold a top with sixteen standard tiles 15cm (6″) square. The chipboard is fractionally larger than the required area to allow for slight variances in tile sizes. Any crevices showing after the tiles are placed in position should be filled with grout. The frame around the chipboard is made with mitre joints but if you find these difficult, butt joints are equally suitable. The materials listed will make a sturdy and easily washable top about 61.5cm (24¼″) square.

You will need:
Softwood 25mm x 12mm (1″ x ½″), 275cm (9′) long—cut into four equal lengths.

3. Assemble and attach the four pieces of timber around the chipboard. To do this glue the strips and secure them with panel pins set below wood surface.

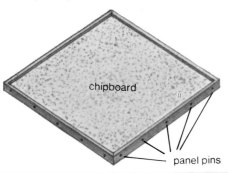

chipboard

panel pins

4. Fill pin holes with wood filler or plastic wood and finish with fine grade sandpaper when dry.

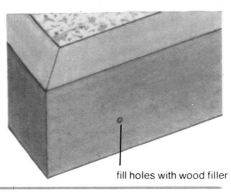

fill holes with wood filler

5. Apply polyurethane varnish or wood stain (as for the underframe) to finish. Cover the wrong side of the chipboard with polyurethane varnish.

6. Drill four holes in the chipboard so that two coincide with each of the two upper cross rails. Mark the cross rails where the holes are and drill pilot holes about 13mm (½″) deep into the cross rails.

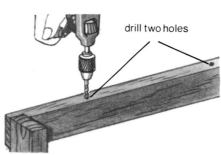

drill two holes

7. Position the chipboard top on the underframe and secure with screws.

8. Stick the tiles in position with the tile adhesive and, after 24 hours, grout the tiles. The grout can be stained the same colour as the table.

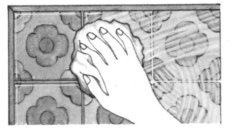

19mm ($\frac{3}{4}''$) chipboard, 61.5cm ($24\frac{1}{4}''$) square—if you already have the tiles, place them in position, measure them, and make any necessary adjustment to the size of the chipboard when purchasing it.

16 tiles 15cm (6″) square, tile adhesive and grout.

Tools as for the underframe. Hardware remaining from the construction of the underframe, ie panel pins and screws.

Woodworking adhesive, woodstain, varnish or paint, depending on the finish you prefer.

Alternative tops

The top for the underframe can be varied in size. A large top, not necessarily square can also be made. Glass can be placed in the frame or use plate glass to cover the frame.

Collages and tapestries. If a collage or tapestry is mounted on to a suitable backing board the chipboard base will not be necessary. Make the frame to fit around the backing board, remove the tapestry or collage and secure the backing board to the underframe. Replace the tapestry or collage and attach the frame with panel pins to the backing board. This makes the top permanent, but you might prefer to use chipboard and lay the tapestry or collage on top of it so that you can change the inlay if you like.

Complete all construction work before you have glass cut for the top so as to ensure that the top fits the frame as accurately as possible.

Display table tops. A frame can be built up to hold three-dimensional objects such as shells, butterflies or semi-precious stones. A simple way of doing this is to use timber, say 75mm x 25mm (3″ x 1″) softwood, with a strip of beading added to hold the glass The frame does not have to be square. If the top overlaps the underframe and it is oblong make sure that the underframe is secured centrally to the top.

Below: a display table top used to house a collection of shells.

49

A modular system for making furniture

Furniture designers, in an attempt to cater for storage needs, developed versatile units which can be arranged to suit almost any setting. Based on the multiples of a simple box, the merit of such systems of storage furniture is their flexibility. They can be adapted without major upheavals to suit the needs of a living-room, bedroom or kitchen while maintaining a visual unity.

The modular unit

This series of chapters shows you how to make a system of storage furniture, based on a simple square module, that can be used throughout the house. The primary module has a square front elevation of 25cm (10″)—ie when viewed from the front. Two opposite sides of this unit can be doubled to form a rectangle. By continuing this doubling up process, larger square and rectangular units are made which can be used in any combination.

As each unit is complete in itself, the system enables you to build up a collection of furniture, unit by unit, according to your needs and budget. The simplicity of the design and number of possible variations enable the units to blend with almost any setting.

The basic construction of the module is the same for all the units, regardless of size. They can be either wall hung or free standing arrangements; combinations of both enable each unit to be built up to the height best suited for its purpose.

Materials

In order to keep costs at a reasonable level, the units can be made from chipboard, pre-veneered in either wood or plastic finish. A pre-veneered plastic

The measurements used in the construction of the modular furniture are given in metric only. This is necessary because a convenient size had to be decided on for the design of the units. Overall dimensions will be given in both metric and imperial to give an idea of the finished size of the units.

finish, such as Contiplas, is more practical for bathrooms, kitchen surfaces and children's playrooms because it is durable and easy to clean.

A pre-veneered chipboard, such as Contiboard, offers a wide selection of wood finishes. Contiboard is sold in sheets of 183cm (6′) and 244cm (8′) lengths and a number of widths, ranging from 152mm (6″) to 914mm (36″). The long edges are lipped, ie the surface finish is carried over to the edge. Matching veneer strips can be bought for finishing cut edges.

All the units illustrated in these chapters have been made from Contiboard 16mm ($\frac{5}{8}$″) thick. The battens can be stained or painted the required colour.

Finishes

If using a raw or unfinished chipboard the surface and edges must be sanded to a smooth finish. Cheaper grades of chipboard tend to have a crumbly core and cut edges will need filling with a proprietary cellulose filler before painting. When painting, always apply a suitable primer, undercoat and one or two topcoats.

Wood veneer boards can be rubbed along the grain with a fine grade glasspaper and then coated with a clear varnish to bring out the natural colour of the veneer. A colour stain can also be applied should you want to change the appearance of the wood.

Veneer chipboards, such as Contiboard, are available in 'white wood' (pine), teak, mahogany and sapele.

Planning

An important aspect of installing furniture is making sure it is both convenient and comfortable to use. The most carefully laid out cupboard interior will be of little value if the whole unit is so placed that its interior and contents are inaccessible.

An arrangement of modular unit furniture making use of both wall hung and free standing units. The units are made from natural teak veneer chipboard which has been finished with clear varnish. The units are all based on the basic unit described in this chapter. The larger units are dealt with later. Designed by Jackson Day Designs.

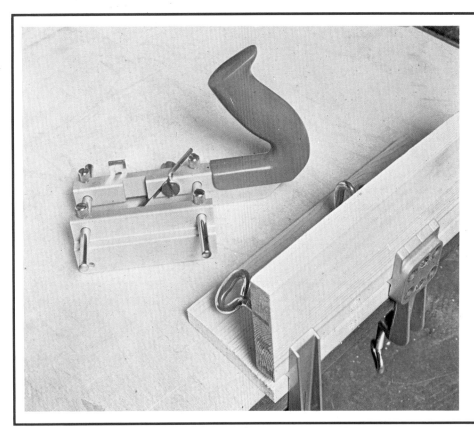

Tool box

Plough plane. This is a useful special-purpose plane used for planing grooves. The plane has an adjustable side arm, known as the fence, which is used to determine how far in from the wood's edge the groove is to be cut. The depth of the groove is controlled by an adjustable depth gauge attached to the main body of the plane.

When ploughing, always keep the plane vertical and the fence pressed flat against the side of the wood. Start the groove at the furthest point away from you and gradually work your way backwards.

Dowelling jig. The jig enables you to position holes for dowel joints accurately. It has two clamps, one which holds the wood in position. The other clamp has three pairs of holes in it and is positioned so the required holes are over the places for the dowels. The holes are then drilled using the holes in the clamp to guide the drill bit.

Construction

To introduce the construction techniques the basic unit is built (fig.1a). It is 25cm (10″) square and 22.9cm (9″) deep.

You will need:

Four pieces 16mm thick chipboard, 21.8cm long x 229mm wide. (Two boxes can be cut from one piece of chipboard 183cm long and 229mm wide.)

Four ramin battens, 16mm x 16mm and 22.9cm long. Ramin is a hard and close-textured timber with a clear, even grain.

60cm of 6mm dowelling.

One piece 3mm hardboard, 22.4cm x 22.4cm—for the back panel.

2 pieces softwood 38mm x 12mm and 21.8cm long, for wall mounting.

White woodworking adhesive.

Tools:

Panel saw or circular saw attachment and tenon saw.

Carpenter's square, trimming knife, spirit level and pencil.

Drill with 6mm wood bit and No.8 masonry bit.

Plough plane and dowelling jig.

☐ Have the chipboard cut to the required size by the timber merchant.

If you are cutting the board, allow about 2mm for each saw cut.

Note: a scored line made with a marking knife prevents the surface splitting when being cut.

☐ Mark the centres for the two pairs of dowels on each batten (fig.1b).

☐ Using a dowelling jig and a drill with a 6mm wood bit, make holes 9mm deep in the battens and 16mm in the chipboard edge to correspond with the holes in the battens.

☐ A back panel can be fitted, especially if the unit is wall hung. This is made from 3mm hardboard held in place in

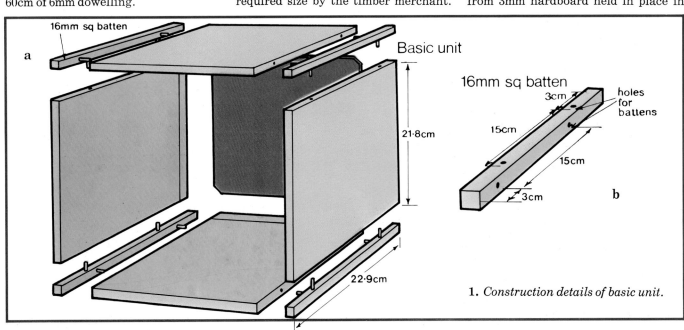

Basic unit

21·8cm

22·9cm

16mm sq batten

16mm sq batten

3cm

holes for battens

15cm

15cm

3cm

b

a

1. Construction details of basic unit.

a groove 3mm deep cut on inside face of the panels, 12mm from the back edge. Use a plough plane or circular saw. If the latter is used and depending on the thickness of the blade, two cuts will probably have to be made, adjusting the blade guide with each cut to produce the required width of groove. The timber merchant from whom you buy the chipboard may be prepared to cut these grooves.

☐ Cut off 7mm from the corners of the back panel (see fig.1a).

☐ Lightly sand the battens and panels. Where necessary finish exposed chipboard edges with a suitable veneer strip or filler. Avoid getting paint or varnish on those edges to be glued.

☐ Paint or varnish the smooth surface of the hardboard back and allow to dry.

☐ Cut 16 pieces of 6mm dowel, each 2.5cm long. Glue a dowel in each of the holes drilled in the battens.

☐ Apply white woodworking adhesive to the dowelled edges of the battens and on the protruding dowels.

☐ Assemble three sides of the box, fitting the dowels into the corresponding holes on the edge of the board (see detail in fig.1a).

☐ Slide in the back panel, smooth side facing inwards and fix final side of box.

☐ Cramp the box together using sash cramps or make your own cramps by cutting right-angle corner blocks held in place by a double loop of cord (fig.2).

☐ Check with the carpenter's square that the box is square or by measuring the diagonals—if both diagonals are equal the corners form right angles.

Partitions. Fit small screw eyes in two opposite sides of the unit (fig.3). Lay a piece of 3mm hardboard 21.8cm x 21.4cm on top to form a shelf. These partitions are optional.

Mounting

To fix to a wall, cut two 38mm x 12mm battens, 21.8cm long, from softwood.

☐ Plane or cut a 45° bevel on one long edge of each. Position as shown in fig.4 and plane flush if necessary.

☐ Drill and countersink one batten to take two screws, 5cm from each end.

The units can be finished to suit particular settings. Here, they have been painted brightly and used for general storage in a children's room.

☐ Screw the batten to the wall at the desired height with two 5cm No.8 countersunk screws. Check with a spirit level that it is horizontal.

☐ Glue the other batten to the underneath of the top panel, behind the back panel. The bevel should face inwards (fig.4).

☐ The box is simply hung on the batten (see fig.4).

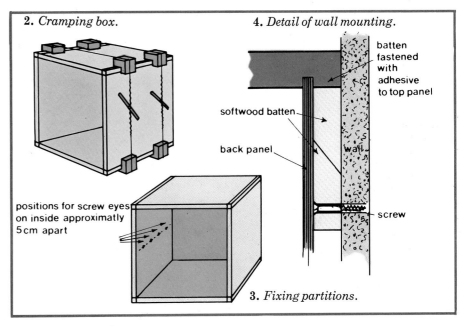

2. *Cramping box.*

positions for screw eyes on inside approximatly 5cm apart

3. *Fixing partitions.*

4. *Detail of wall mounting.*

batten fastened with adhesive to top panel

softwood batten

back panel

wall

screw

Wall-hung desk with matching shelves

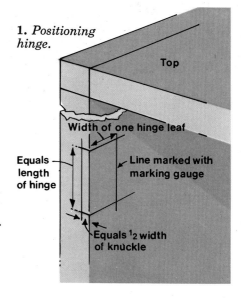

1. *Positioning hinge.*

Top

Width of one hinge leaf

Equals length of hinge

Line marked with marking gauge

Equals ½ width of knuckle

Once you have mastered the technique of building the primary unit, then the rest of the modular unit furniture system becomes relatively easy, even for the beginner. While keeping the square profile of the units, you can increase the size and vary the depth for a wider range of storage furniture.

This chapter describes the construction of a wall-hung desk which can be used as a dressing-table or a work area in a teenager's room or study. The unit is developed with the addition of doors.

Fitting doors

A number of different types of doors can be fitted to any unit, the simplest being a panel of 16mm chipboard cut to the required size.

Basically there are two ways of hanging a door: in one the door is inset, ie fits flush within the carcass (framework) of the unit. In the other, known as lay-on, the door fits on the carcass.

Inset doors

The inset door is more difficult to fit than the lay-on as it requires careful measuring and cutting to ensure that it does not stick or look badly fitted. The advantage of the inset door is that it makes use of inexpensive and widely available butt hinges (see box).

You will need:

16mm pre-veneered chipboard for door —size as required.

Butt hinges with an open width of 2.5cm—two for each door.

Chipboard screws to fit hinges.

12mm bevel edge chisel.

Screwdriver, wooden mallet, marking gauge, pencil and ruler.

Drill and suitably sized drill bits.

☐ To fit an inset door, take the inside measurements of the box and cut the door slightly smaller to fit.

☐ Position the door inside the carcass so that it fits flush with the edges. Raise the door slightly with cardboard or thin pieces of wood so that it stands in its correct position.

☐ Make a pencil mark on the door and carcass 8cm from the top of the door. Repeat at the bottom.

☐ Remove the door. Set a marking gauge to half the thickness of the hinge knuckle and mark a line on the facing side of the door and carcass edge (fig.1).

☐ Set the marking gauge to the width of one hinge leaf and mark out on edge of door and side of carcass (see fig.1).

☐ Use a pencil to mark the length of the hinge. The top of the upper hinge coincides with the top line drawn earlier and the bottom of the lower hinge with the other.

☐ Use a chisel to cut round the outline of each hinge leaf (fig.2). Chisel out waste wood to leave a neat, flat-bottomed recess into which the hinge fits in it. Repeat the procedure on the door. **Note:** make the recess too shallow rather than too deep as it can always be cut deeper to allow the hinge leaf to lie flush in it.

☐ When the hinge leaves fit neatly, drill one hole through the centre hole of each hinge leaf into the door and carcass. Do not drill the other two holes in each side leaf yet.

☐ Mount the door, fixing it temporarily with one screw in each hinge leaf.

☐ Test to see whether the door opens and closes freely. Make any necessary adjustments. Mark the remaining screw holes. Drill the holes and insert screws.

Make sure that the screws are sunk well into the hinge or they will prevent the door closing properly.

2. *Cutting out hinge recess.*

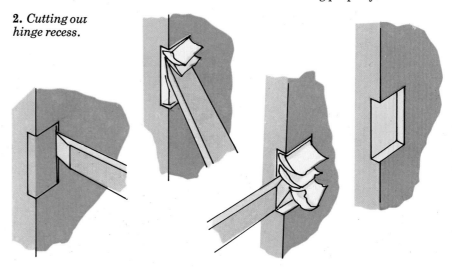

Lay-on doors

The same procedure is followed as for the inset door except that in this case the hinge fits into the *edge* of the carcass rather than the side.

The lay-on door, though easier to fit, requires a cranked or angle hinge which will lift the door clear of the neighbouring door (see box overleaf).

You will need:

Cranked or angle hinges with flaps no wider than 12mm—two for each door. For doors on the larger cupboards (200cm tall) use three hinges.

16mm chipboard for door—size as required. Tools as for the inset door.

☐ Cut the lay-on door 3mm smaller all round than the front outline of the carcass. This serves as a design feature, creating a thin 'shadow' line between each cupboard door. It also allows room for the doors to swing clear.

☐ Follow the same procedures described for the inset door, bearing in mind that the hinge is recessed into the edge of the door. The hinged doors can now be fitted with catches and handles (see box overleaf).

Two large wall-hung units with an attached work surface forming a desk. Designed by Jackson Day Designs.

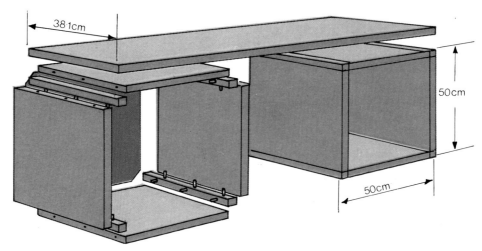

3a. *Construction diagram of desk with exploded view of one unit.*

38.1cm

50cm

50cm

Desk

The desk is comprised of two square units 50cm x 50cm (20″x 20″) with a depth of 38.1cm (15″). Chipboard is placed across the two units (fig.3a) to form a work surface 150cm (59″) long. The instructions are for a wall-mounted desk. For a free-standing desk adapt two units to a size suitable for lifting the work surface to the required level, 70cm (2′4″) being a recommended height for a desk top.

The unit can be adapted to other uses as well and the depth can vary accordingly.

A work surface for a study table or sewing area should be larger than a dresser. Decide on a size to suit your own particular requirements.

You will need:

Eight 16mm chipboard panels 46.8cm long and the required depth, in this case 38.1cm—for the two units.

Eight pieces 16mm x 16mm ramin batten, same length as depth of units.

Two pieces 3mm hardboard, 47.4cm square—for back panels.

One piece 16mm chipboard, 150cm long and 381mm wide—for the work surface.

Four pieces softwood, 38mm x 15mm and 46.8cm long—with bevelled edges for wall mounting (see Carpentry chapter 24, page 2250).

6mm dowelling—enough for all the joints.

No.6 chipboard screws 25mm long—for securing work surface.

Masonry screws—see previous chapter.

Tools—as for previous chapter.

☐ Construct the two identical modular units according to the standard method already described. The spacings for the dowel pegs on the battens are shown in fig. 3b.

☐ Fit the bevel edged softwood for the wall mounts.

☐ Mount the units to the wall, 50cm apart and level with each other.

Open shelves

Shelves can be fitted above the desk. Various means of securing shelves have already been dealt with, but here the instructions given are for a single shelf using keyhole plates.

You will need:

16mm chipboard 46.8cm long and 229mm wide. This size is relevant to the desk but you can adapt it to suit yourself.

Two 16mm x 16mm ramin battens, 22.9cm long.

Two pieces 16mm chipboard 12.8cm long and 229mm wide—for the two ends.

Two keyhole plates—for fastening shelves to wall (fig.4).

Length of 6mm dowelling.

Two coverhead wood screws.

No.8 round head screws 50mm long for wall.

Rawlplugs for wall.

☐ Fit the keyhole plates to the back edges of the end pieces, 2cm down from the top (see fig.4).

☐ Join the ends to the shelf using the battens and dowelling.

☐ Fit two coverhead screws in back edge of shelf, 5cm from each end (see inset, fig.4). These are screwed in or out to adjust the shelf to the wall level.

☐ Measure the distance between the centres of the keyslotted plates, mark

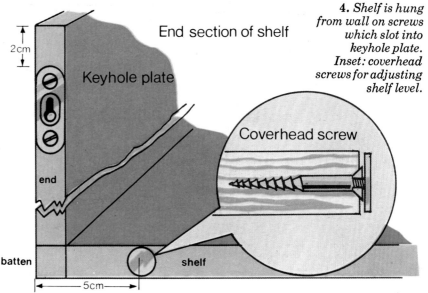

2cm

End section of shelf

Keyhole plate

end

batten

shelf

5cm

4. *Shelf is hung from wall on screws which slot into keyhole plate. Inset: coverhead screws for adjusting shelf level.*

Coverhead screw

the wall with this length at the required height. Check the level with a spirit level and drill and plug the wall. The heads of the screws should project about 3mm from the wall.

☐ Hang the shelves on No.8 round head screws.

Plinth

If a series of floor-standing units is required, they should be placed on a

plinth (fig.5). This will correct any misalignment due to uneven floors and keep the doors and drawers clear of the carpet. Make the plinth the overall length of units to ensure that they are all on the same level.

To make a plinth, measure the total width of the units and cut the front and back rails of the plinth from 50mm x 25mm softwood to this length. Cut the side rails 25mm shorter than the depth

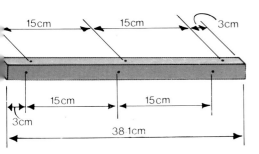

15cm   15cm   3cm

15cm   15cm

3cm

38.1cm

3b. *Positions for dowels on batten.*

☐ Place the chipboard for the work surface across the tops of the two units forming a knee hole.

☐ Fix the work surface to the units with countersunk screws driven up through the top of the boxes.

A larger desk with a wider knee hole will need rails across the underside of the work surface.

To do this, measure the width between the units and cut two rails from 50mm x 25mm softwood to required length. Glue and screw these rails to the underside of the work surface, 38mm in from the front and back edges. This serves to prevent the surface sagging.

Top view of plinth

50mm x 25mm softwood frame mitred at corners fitted with corner blocks

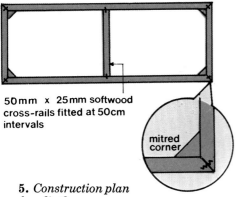

50mm x 25mm softwood cross-rails fitted at 50cm intervals

mitred corner

5. *Construction plan for plinth.*

of the unit. Mitre corners, pin and glue. Fit corner blocks to reinforce joints.

Add a centre cross-rail for every unit or at intervals of 50cm. Finish to match units. Use spirit level to check evenness of plinth and, if necessary, plane off excess timber.

Mobile boxes can be made by simply screwing on plate-fixed castors to the bottom of the unit.

Hardware
Hinges

There are numerous types of hinges available. However, a butt hinge and an angle or crank hinge is all that is required for inset or lay-on doors. The butt hinge is the most common hinge and is used on an inset door. The angle or crank hinge is used on a lay-on door because it is designed to lift the door clear of adjacent doors.

Catches

Having hinged the door, it has to be fitted with a catch or lock to keep it closed. One of the simplest means of securing a cabinet door is to fit a magnetic catch. This consists of a plastic mounting containing a magnet (usually sprung to take up any misalignment) and a metal sticker plate.

The mount is screwed to the inside of the carcass and the plate to the back of the door, in line with the mount.

When fitting a catch it is advisable to place it near the handle. The force applied when opening the door will tend to twist it if positioned off centre. This is most noticeable on long doors.

A catch that does not require a handle, is the auto-latch. To open the door one simply presses it slightly to release the spring mechanism.

There is a variety of catches available from hardware stores and you should find it easy to obtain one suited to your needs.

Handles

There are a number of handles that can be fitted, both plain and fancy, and the final decision is a matter of personal choice.

To make a simple inexpensive handle for both inset and lay-on doors, drill a 2.5cm (1″) hole through the door. Round off the edges with glasspaper and finish with a stain or paint to match the door. Another cut-out type of handle is made by cutting a 5cm (2″) wide semi-circle in the edge of the door. The cut edge can be finished with strips of veneer which are then trimmed and sanded. This handle is only suitable for inset doors.

If a knob is wanted, cut a 3.8cm length of 18mm dowel and glue it into an 18mm deep hole in the face of the door.

Screw-in type handles are also available—the choice really depends on the appearance you prefer.

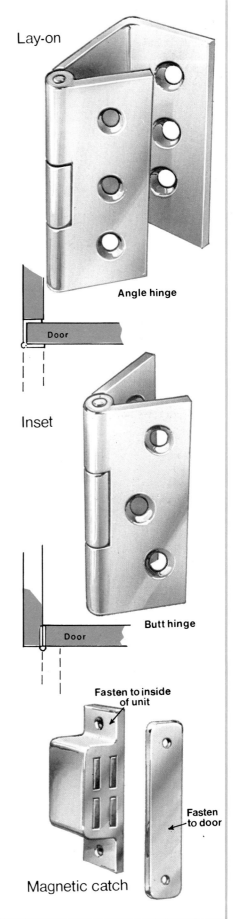

Lay-on

Angle hinge

Door

Inset

Butt hinge

Door

Fasten to inside of unit

Fasten to door

Magnetic catch

Adding drawers to the modular system

Drawers are one of the most economical and practical ways of utilizing the space in the larger units of the modular system. All drawers consist basically of a four-sided frame with runners on which the drawer slides. The frame is fitted with a base usually of a thinner material. The base helps to hold the frame square as the sides of the drawer must be parallel to operate properly.

The runners, which can be either cleated or recessed (fig.1a and b), must also be parallel to the runners fitted on the sides of the carcass. Great care must be taken with this aspect of construction in order to make a successful drawer.

Drawer fronts. These can be of two shapes: lay-on (also known as over-width) and inset as shown in fig.1a and b. The inset front drawer is a plain box with all the corners and edges flush. Because the front does not project beyond the sides, any inaccuracy in the fitting of the drawer runners will show. The lay-on front is more generally used on modern furniture. If using the three-cleat technique (see fig.1a), always use the lay-on front as the front projects to conceal the runners.

Three-cleat technique. A cleat (wood or plastic strip) is fitted to the centre of each drawer side. Two parallel cleats are attached to each side of the carcass, into which the cleat on the drawer slides (see fig.1a).

The technique is not suitable for very wide and heavy drawers as all the weight is taken on the two cleats. The large gap down each side of the drawer accommodating the cleats on the carcass is concealed by lay-on fronts.

Cleat-and-groove technique. Drawers using this technique are harder to build than those with the three cleats. A single cleat is fixed to each side of the unit which fits into a groove cut along the sides of the drawer (see fig.1b). If the groove is made as deep as the thickness of the cleat, the drawer can be made the full width of the space into which it fits. Allowance must be made for shrinkage and/or expansion of the wood. (This, of course, does not apply to ready-made plastic drawer kits.) The groove stops short of the front of the drawer. If the drawer is made entirely from wood, the

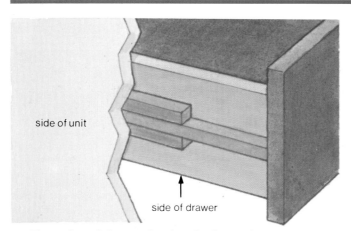

1a. *Three-cleated drawer fitted with a lay-on front.*

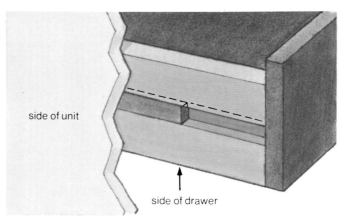

1b. *Cleat-and-groove drawer with an inset front.*

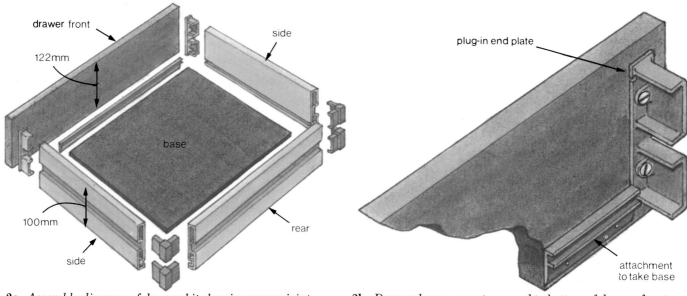

2a. *Assembly diagram of drawer kit showing corner joints.*

2b. *Drawer base support screwed to bottom of drawer front.*

groove must be cut with a plough plane. Because of the problem of friction, chipboard sides are unsuitable for this type of drawer. In order to eliminate the friction problem with drawers, the cleats should be made of hardwood.

In recent years the development of plastic-moulded drawer components has made drawer making a lot easier. There are a number of ready-made drawer kits available, such as Sheerglide, which consist of 200cm (80″) lengths of moulded plastic. These are cut to the required size and joined at corners with special fittings (fig.2a).

Making a drawer

The following instructions are for a lay-on front plastic drawer which operates on the cleat-and-groove technique. The drawer is made to fit a square unit, 50cm x 50cm (20″ x 20″); four drawers each with a side profile of 100mm (4″) can be fitted into a unit this size. When fitting drawers, keep in mind the depth of the unit—short drawers are impractical.

You will need:

Three plastic drawer sides 100mm wide: one 43.7cm long, for back; two 3cm shorter than depth of unit, for sides. Two corner pieces and two plug-in end plates for assembling.

3mm hardboard base 450mm wide and depth 1.2cm longer than sides.

One pair of plastic drawer runners, cut to match length of sides.

Note: for inset drawers reduce the length of sides and depth of base by 20mm.

The drawer front is cut from 16mm thick Contiboard, 49.4cm long x 122mm wide for lay-on drawers (46.5cm x 115mm for inset drawers).

The drawer front is fitted to the sides with plug-in end plates which are screw fixed with chipboard screws to the back

of the drawer front (fig.2b). For each set of four drawers, the bottom edge of the drawer front for the top three drawers is flush with the bottom of the sides. The top of the bottom drawer front is flush with the top of the drawer sides (fig.3).

Before fixing the drawer front, mark a 3mm groove to take the baseboard. This can either be cut with a circular saw, or a special fitting to take the base can be attached to the inside of the front (see fig.2b). Place strips of veneer on the top and ends of the front only.

Position runners or cleats on carcass

A drawer kit with lay-on fronts fitted into a unit 50cm square and 38.1cm deep.

as shown: fig.4a gives positions for three-cleated drawers; fig.4b gives positions for plastic runners and cleat-and-groove drawers with lay-on fronts. Assemble the drawer and check that it fits the carcass. Dismantle, make any necessary alterations and then rebuild, fixing the corner fittings with a small amount of plastic adhesive. Slide the base into place and attach the front of the drawer. Fit or cut handles and finish the drawer front as required.

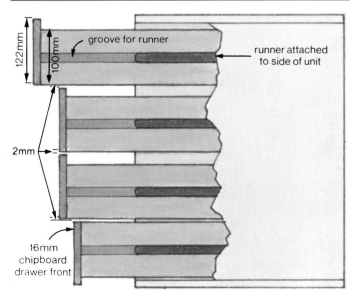

3. *Positioning of drawer fronts in lay-on drawers.*

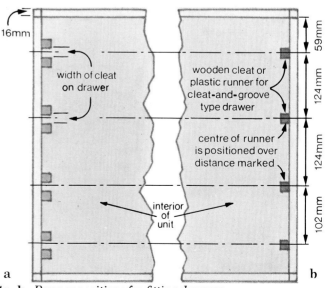

4a, b. *Runner positions for fitting drawers.*

Bedroom wardrobe or kitchen cupboard

By increasing the height of the basic unit in multiples of 50cm (20″) a rectangular unit, 50cm x 200cm (20″ x 79″) can be produced. Made with a depth of 61cm (24″), this unit can be used as a wardrobe in a bedroom. A shallower unit of 38.1cm (15″) could be used in the kitchen. The height of the unit is sufficient to hang clothes or to take brooms and mops.

Wardrobe

The following instructions are for making a wardrobe 61cm deep. The interior can be arranged to make it a full-length hanging cupboard or pull-out shelves can be fitted to take smaller items of clothing. Fig.1 shows two combined units mounted on a plinth.

You will need:
Two pieces of 16mm chipboard, 196.8cm long and 610mm wide—for the sides.
Two pieces 16mm chipboard, 46.8cm long and 610mm wide—for the top and bottom. Four pieces 16mm ramin batten, 61cm long.
6mm dowelling 60cm long.
One piece 16mm chipboard, 199.4cm long and 494mm wide—for lay-on door —or 196.8cm long and 468mm wide— for an inset door.
One piece of 16mm chipboard 46.8cm long and 59.5cm deep—for shelf.
Tools as for previous chapters.
Hinges (see page 57)
Construct the unit following the same

1. *Wardrobe with hanging space.*
2. *Positions on batten for dowels.*
3. *Glide rail for wardrobe.* 4. *Pull-out shelves.* 5. *Kitchen cupboards.* 6. *Packing strip cut to width of runner.*

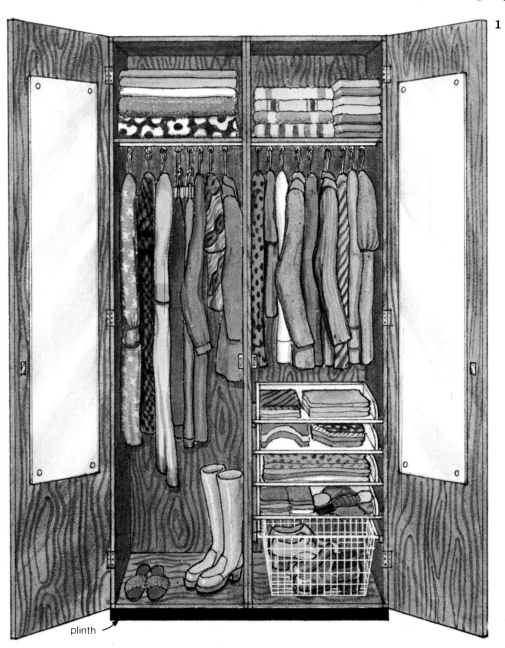

plinth

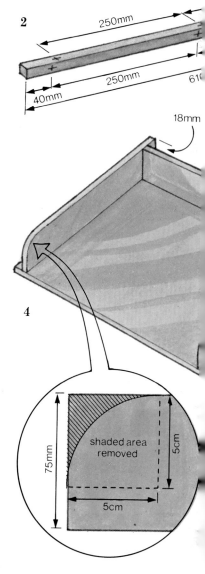

1

2

250mm

250mm

40mm

610

18mm

4

75mm

5cm

shaded area removed

5cm

technique as for the basic square unit already described. The holes in the battens for the dowelling are situated as shown in fig. 2.

A fitted cupboard (fig.1). For this, fix a shelf 36.8cm from the top. Dowel joint the shelf to the cupboard sides using the nylon recessed fitting method or alternatively the screw eye and slot method described in the next chapter. Screw fix a glide rail (fig.3) to the underside of the shelf to carry coat-hangers. The merit of this fitting is that it allows the garments to be slid apart easily when removing or placing them in the cupboard. The upper section of the shelf can be used for hat or blanket storage.

Pull-out shelves. Each shelf consists of a base, two sides and a back. Instructions for making up one shelf are given here. The shelf slides on plastic runners.

You will need:
One piece of 12mm plywood, 59.5cm long and 462mm wide—for the base.
Two pieces 12mm x 75mm softwood, 57.6cm long—for the sides.
One piece 12mm x 75mm softwood, 41cm long—for the back.
Two plastic drawer runners 59.5cm long.
No.8 chipboard screws 1.2cm long.
☐ Screw the runners to the sides of the unit. When fitting a series of shelves fix the runners 13cm apart.
☐ Shape the front ends of the sides as shown in the inset, in fig.4.
☐ Using a butt joint assemble sides and back with glue and pins. The back should be set 1.8cm in from the back of the sides (see fig.4). Then glue and pin the sides and back centrally on to the base with the back ends of the sides flush with the back edge of the base.
☐ Paint or stain as required.

Kitchen cupboard
A kitchen cupboard need not be as deep as the wardrobe. The interior of the cupboard can be adapted according to your needs. A full-length cupboard is ideal for storing brooms, mops and other large items, whereas smaller objects can be housed in storage baskets. Fig.5 shows these two interior layouts.

Storage baskets. Banks of storage baskets can be used in a kitchen cupboard to store dry goods. The baskets come in two depths, 23cm and 10cm, and are available from a number of firms.

To fit a wire basket 10cm deep, screw fix plastic drawer runners, 59.5cm long and 13cm apart, to the sides of the cupboard, packing the runners out from the sides with a strip of 6mm plywood (fig.6). The top edges of the wire basket run freely in the plastic runner.

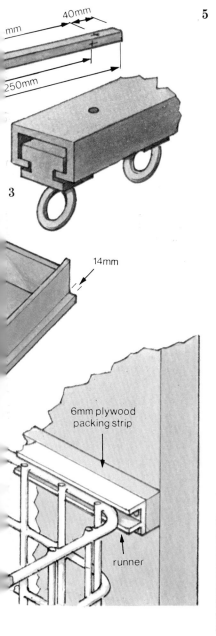

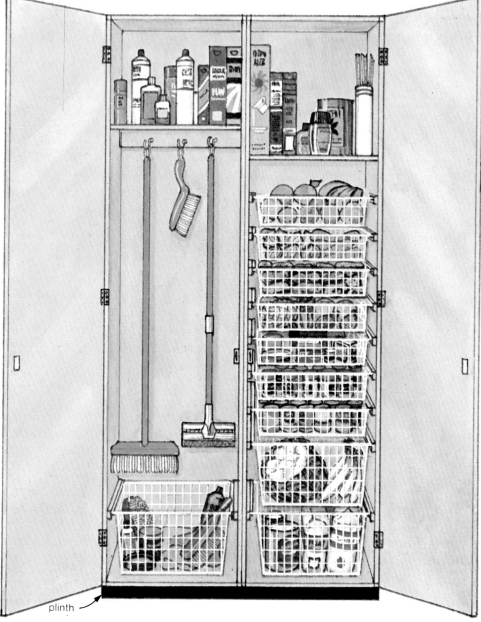

5